MAKING NUMBER TALKS MATTER

Developing Mathematical Practices and Deepening Understanding,

GRADES 4-10

CATHY HUMPHREYS & RUTH PARKER

FOREWORD BY JO BOALER

Stenhouse Publishers
www.stenhouse.com

Library of Congress Cataloging-in-Publication Data
Humphreys, Cathy.

Making number talks matter : developing mathematical practices and deepening understanding, grades 4-10 / Cathy Humphreys and Ruth Parker ; foreword by Jo Boaler.

p.   cm.

Includes bibliographical references and index.
ISBN 978-1-57110-998-9 (pbk. : alk. paper)
ISBN 978-1-62531-019-4 (ebook)
1. Mathematics--Study and teaching (Elementary)
2. Mathematics--Study and teaching
(Middle school) I. Parker, Ruth E. II. Title.

QA135.6.H857 2015

510.71'2--dc23

2014044584

Cover design by Blue Design. Interior design and typesetting by Victory Productions, Inc.

Manufactured in the United States of America

PRINTED ON 30% PCW
RECYCLED PAPER

21 20 19 18 17 16 15   9 8 7 6 5 4

To Ellie and Ezra (and Cathy's little ones yet to come) — you're the inspiration for our work and give us hope for the future.

Contents

Foreword: The Wonder of Number Talks

Number Talks are the perfect start to any math class. They are like no other teaching method I know. Many important math activities require a lot of planning and an hour of teaching time, but Number Talks are different. In a really short span of time (fifteen minutes or so), teachers can provide students with some of the greatest opportunities—they can change their view of mathematics, teach them number sense, help them develop mental math skills, and, at the same time, engage them in creative, open mathematics. I taught Number Talks in my online class for teachers (www.youcubed.org), which was taken by 40,000 people. Since then, teachers of all grade levels have been telling me that Number Talks have changed everything for their students. How fantastic then that Cathy Humphreys and Ruth Parker, two of the greatest practitioners I know, who have wisdom about mathematics learning that is deeper than almost anyone I have ever met, have teamed up to write this book.

Ruth Parker and Kathy Richardson created Number Talks in the early 1990s, although few people know this fact. Cathy Humphreys has been instrumental in extending Number Talks to the secondary level and has studied their use with high school students as well as with graduate students at Stanford University. Together, Cathy and Ruth have developed incredible knowledge of the best ways to teach Number Talks with students of all grade levels. That knowledge is packed into this highly readable book.

One of the reasons Number Talks are so important is that they give students, and adults, a whole different perspective on mathematics—a perspective that turns out to be critical for future learning. In recent years, I was teaching a group of disaffected seventh- and eighth-grade students (Boaler 2015) with my graduate students at Stanford, in the challenging context of summer school. Most of the students hated math, and their only experience of math learning had been silently computing problems on worksheets—hence their dislike of the subject. We started each day of the summer with a Number Talk and collected students' different methods for solving the day's particular problems. This experience was transformative for the students because they had never before realized that math problems could be solved in different ways, particularly bare number problems such as 27 $\times$ 12. During their time with us, the students learned that mathematics is an open and visual subject and that all math problems can be solved using different methods and pathways. This new perspective changed everything for the students, and we could not have achieved this important shift without Number Talks.

Since learning about Number Talks from Ruth and Cathy, I have used them in many different situations, working on the exact same problems with undergraduates at Stanford University, struggling schoolchildren, and CEOs of major companies—all with equally high engagement. I have learned through this process that even high-level mathematics users, including those working at top firms such as Wolfram Alpha and Udacity, did not know that number problems could be so open, with solutions that are creative and can be shown visually. One reader of my book *What's Math Got to Do with It?*, which shows several methods to solve the problem 18 $\times$ 5, said she had known that number problems have different methods but somehow had always thought that creative and flexible solutions were "against the rules" in mathematics.

The power of Number Talks to transform people's views of mathematics cannot be overstated, but there are other important goals that also can be achieved. Number sense is the most important foundation that students can have and the basis for all higher-level mathematics. When students fail algebra, it is not because algebra is a really hard subject; it is because they do not have a foundation of number sense. Although many teachers understand this, they do not know how to develop number sense in students and often work *against* number sense by encouraging the rote memorization of number facts and procedures (Boaler 2014). When any teacher asks me, "How do I develop number sense?" my answer is short: Number Talks. As well as teaching students the math facts that they need to know, Number Talks teach students to understand the numerical relationships that are so critical to understanding mathematics. They also help teachers create classrooms in which students feel encouraged to share their thinking, and teachers become skilled at listening to their students' thinking. These are some of the most important goals for any mathematics classroom.

Number Talks are highly learnable, and very enjoyable for teachers to enact, but there are important things to know about how to implement them most effectively. Teachers can watch a video of an expert teacher giving a Number Talk and believe that they are simple to teach, because they can *appear* deceptively easy. Yet when teachers begin to teach Number Talks themselves, many questions arise: What do they say when students share an incorrect solution, or when there is a mistake in their work? What do teachers do when students have no methods to share? How do teachers know the best problems to use for Number Talks? Where do they find examples of Number Talks for middle and high school students? These questions, and many more, are answered in this book.

I find books written by real teachers, describing the craft of teaching, fascinating. I love to read about the complexity of teaching and the decisions teachers make in supporting their students' learning. *Making Number Talks Matter* was a particular treat for me to read because it delves deeply into teaching, describing students' mathematical strategies as well as different pedagogical strategies, including those that can be used in the hardest teaching situations. The rich knowledge that Cathy and Ruth share, drawing from decades of experience, is invaluable. I invite you to enjoy the pages that follow, learn from these two amazing educators, and engage students in the wonder of Number Talks.

Jo Boaler, Professor of Mathematics Education, Stanford University

References

Boaler, Jo. 2014. "Fluency Without Fear: Research Evidence on the Best Ways to Learn Math Facts." http://youcubed.org/teachers/wp-content/uploads/2014/10/ FluencyWithoutFear.pdf.

———. 2015. *What's Math Got to Do with It?: How Teachers and Parents Can Transform Mathematics Learning and Inspire Success*. New York: Penguin.

Acknowledgments

This book embodies the deeply held beliefs about teaching and learning that we have developed with the help of the many colleagues, teachers, and students who have challenged and inspired us over the years.

We could not have asked for a better fellow traveler along the way than Patty Lofgren, who has been a true colleague in conceiving, designing, and helping our work with teachers take root. We are indebted to Marilyn Burns, who, so many years ago, believed in us before we believed in ourselves and pushed us to place sense-making at the heart of our teaching. We are also grateful to Joan Carlson for showing us the magic that happens when we pose problems, get out of the way, and let kids struggle to make sense. And we are especially thankful to Bonnie Tank for sharing with us her wisdom about engaging teachers and students with mathematical ideas and for inspiring us to do the same.

Toby Gordon, thank you for inviting us to write, gently checking in to see how we were doing, and answering "yes" even when our requests were unreasonable. You knew what we were trying to do and helped us do it. We couldn't have asked for a better editor and mentor.

Dan Tobin, we are eternally grateful for your efforts to help get our work on Number Talks out into the world.

And finally, we want to thank the many teachers and colleagues who nudged us to "hurry up and write."

Cathy:
It has been amazing to write this book with Ruth, who has long been my hero and has inspired me in so many ways, and from whom I first learned about Number Talks. I am privileged to have had this experience and glad that I could help her get these important ideas into the hands of more teachers.

So many people have influenced and inspired my professional path! But for this book, I am especially indebted to Melissa Johnson and Tara Perea, who learned to teach Number Talks under the watchful eye of a video camera as we worked together to figure out how to help high school students make sense of all the arithmetic they had learned but little understood. Thank you both for patiently and gracefully answering my many questions and e-mails even these years later. I am also grateful to Jessica Uy and David Heinke—Tara and Melissa's Cooperating Teachers from the Stanford Teacher Education Program—who gave us space and time to learn from their students.

And finally, Sean and Arielle—you mean the world to me!

Ruth:

I'm so very grateful to Kathy Richardson, my good friend and colleague, for the long walks and the many, many hours of conversation that resulted in the birth of what she first came to call "Number Talks." I am especially indebted to Cathy Young for the gift she gave of welcoming me into her classroom for a year. The work we did together to figure out how to bring numerical reasoning and all of mathematics to life with her twenty-nine students forever changed my work.

Cathy, it is an understatement to say that this book would never have been written without you. Your brilliance, gentleness, wisdom, giftedness as a writer, and constant encouragement made you the perfect coauthor. I feel honored to have worked with you. Thank you for saying, "You need to write this book, and I'll write it with you," and never wavering from that commitment.

Finally, Adonia and Ian, you blessed me with two amazing grandchildren who light up my life, and you take such good care of me that I have the time and space to do my work; "thank you" seems inadequate. I love you.

Introduction

Most upper-grade teachers lament their students' lack of mathematical understanding. They often secretly—or not so secretly—wonder what students did in their previous classes. Why don't they know their multiplication facts in fourth, fifth, or even tenth grade? Why do some students still hide their fingers under the table as they count? And why do they have so much trouble with fractions? The fact that this happens in so many classrooms across the country tells us that the failure lies not with the students or even their teachers, but in how mathematics has been taught, year after year, with the best of intentions.

Understanding quantities and numerical relationships is within the grasp of all students, yet many of them don't realize it. Students come to classrooms fearing and avoiding math and, worse, thinking they are no good at it. Believing that mathematics is mostly about using procedures correctly, they have learned to focus on getting the right answer, whether or not the process makes sense to them. Many students don't expect math to make sense at all. The result is that students learn to disengage their reasoning—and even distrust it.

Making Number Talks Matter is about helping students take back the authority of their own reasoning through a short, fifteen-minute daily routine called Number Talks, in which they reason mentally with numbers. This book will help you, their teacher, learn how to facilitate this routine so that, over time, students develop a strong sense of the meaning of quantities and operations while gaining proficiency with mathematical practices.

The good news is that Number Talks have a predictable structure that will support you in this rewarding path, no matter what grade you teach. The bad news is that there is not one set route to follow. We can't tell you exactly what to do, and we wouldn't want to even if we could! The process of engaging students in reasoning with numbers is one we hope you will consider as a problem-solving venture—an investigation that will help you learn to listen to your students and learn along with them as you build your lessons around their thinking.

A Word About Us—Cathy and Ruth

Number Talks represented a big change in our own practice. We were both taught to make sure that our students were not confused and to explain clearly and structure our teaching so that students would know just what to do. Coming to know that cognitive dissonance is a valuable and even necessary part of the process of learning caused us to examine our practice on many levels. And the payoff has been huge. As our students came to know that they had mathematical ideas worth listening to, as they learned to defend their ways of knowing with sound mathematical arguments, and as they learned the value of listening to one another and building on the ideas of their peers, the culture of our mathematics classes was richly enhanced.

Yes, we focus on Number Talks in *Making Number Talks Matter*, but we also take time to explore principles of teaching and learning. We would love to see every classroom every day be guided by the principles we've outlined here. And we know that providing a space where for fifteen minutes a day children can be the "havers" of mathematical ideas—just this one small innovation—can profoundly change students' relationship with mathematics and their belief about themselves as learners. Ultimately, if enough students start believing in themselves, it just might change the world.

What follows is a quick overview of each chapter. While we hope that you will find the entire book to be both motivating and helpful, we are aware that readers bring a wide range of experience when it comes to Number Talks. For those of you who are new to Number Talks, we have tried to provide enough detail so that you will feel prepared to launch Number Talks in your classrooms. For those of you with a great deal of experience, we hope that we have addressed issues in ways that will help you make Number Talks an even more powerful and empowering part of your school day. The following chapter overviews are intended to help you make decisions about where to begin.

Chapter 1: What Are Number Talks? Why Are They So Important?

Number Talks help bring interest, excitement, and joy back into our mathematics classrooms. Before we show you how to make the short, daily Number Talks a regular part of your classes, we first examine why Number Talks are sorely needed.

Chapter 2: Getting Number Talks Started

Although Number Talks, sometimes called "math talks," are gaining prominence in today's literature and in many classrooms throughout the country, the term means different things to different people. In this chapter, we describe what we mean by Number Talks and explain how to set them up as a class routine. We also suggest teaching strategies and ideas to help your Number Talks be successful.

Chapter 3: Guiding Principles for Enacting Number Talks in the Classroom

Several core beliefs guide all of our teaching decisions during Number Talks. We hope these "Guiding Principles for Number Talks" will become part of your teaching, too.

Prelude to the Operations

Before looking in depth at a particular operation, as we will do in Chapters 4 through 7, we explain how these four chapters are organized. We also introduce three ideas that we consider to be the "new basics" for Number Talks and address issues that are common across the operations of addition, subtraction, multiplication, and division.

Chapter 4: Subtraction Across the Grades

In this chapter, we discuss why subtraction might be a good place to start incorporating Number Talks. We describe the main strategies that work efficiently for subtraction as it deepens in complexity across the grades, and we help you consider why you might choose one problem instead of another.

Chapter 5: Multiplication Across the Grades

This chapter takes us from early multiplication to multidigit multiplication of whole numbers and rational numbers and multiplication of algebraic expressions. We also pay close attention to geometric representations, which are particularly powerful in the transition to algebra.

Chapter 6: Addition Across the Grades

In this chapter we describe and develop strategies that work efficiently for addition as it deepens in complexity across the grades. As with the previous chapters, we also explore the arithmetic properties as they arise in students' methods of solving problems.

Chapter 7: Division Across the Grades

Number Talks can offer a refreshing alternative to teaching the standard long-division algorithm that has long confounded many students while consuming unreasonable amounts of mathematics instruction time. In this chapter, we discuss ways that students can make sense of division, divide integers and rational numbers efficiently, and make reasonable estimates in division.

Chapter 8: Making Sense of Fractions (and Decimals and Percent)

Many middle and high school students want nothing to do with fractions, but their lack of understanding is an obstacle to success in higher mathematics courses. In this chapter, we offer tasks and ideas to help students make sense of fractions, decimals, and percent through Number Talks.

Chapter 9: Number Talks Can Spark Investigations

While it is important to limit daily Number Talks to about fifteen minutes, sometimes a mathematical idea worthy of further investigation arises during a Number Talk. In this chapter we illustrate how ideas posed during Number Talks can lead to important—albeit longer—mathematics lessons.

Chapter 10: Managing Bumps in the Road

As carefully as you might plan, and as much as you believe that Number Talks are important for your students, things won't always go smoothly. You and your students are learning together, so there are bound to be rough patches along the way. But as you will see, these inevitable rough spots offer great opportunities for learning. In this chapter, we identify thorny questions we've been asked, and we share our thoughts on what teachers can do to get beyond some of the common challenges we've all faced with Number Talks.

Chapter 11: Moving Forward

Here we return to our vision in the hopes of inspiring you to continue with what we believe is a transformative classroom practice.

1

What Are Number Talks? Why Are They So Important?

Many teachers have embraced Number Talks, a brief daily practice where students mentally solve computation problems and talk about their strategies, as a way to dramatically transform teaching and learning in their mathematics classrooms. Something wonderful happens when students learn they can make sense of mathematics in their own ways, make mathematically convincing arguments, and critique and build on the ideas of their peers. As students sit on the edge of their seats, eager to share their ideas, digging deep into why mathematical procedures work, they come to like mathematics and know that they can understand it. And while middle and high school students may not demonstrate such overt enthusiasm, they also come to see Number Talks as both meaningful and fun. Teachers soon find out that if they don't make time for a Number Talk, students will remind them. Students don't want to miss Number Talks!

This is a far cry from the mathematics classrooms that most of us experienced, and even quite different from the mathematics classrooms that many of us taught in for years. We have all seen students with their heads on their desks, rubbing their foreheads, or avoiding eye contact to avoid being called on—or even acting out in other ways when they can't access the mathematical ideas. We have also seen the common mistakes that recur year after year as students try, but often fail, to remember the arithmetic rules they have been taught.

Over the past two decades, many of us who have been teaching a long time have felt the very real pressure to put aside what we know makes sense for students and instead teach the procedures students will need for the tests. In the process, too many teachers have lost their love of teaching. It's time to bring joy back into our teaching and into our mathematics class-rooms. Number Talks can be a wonderful vehicle for helping us do this.

This book is about helping teachers learn to make Number Talks matter for their students. It is about helping students learn to work flexibly with numbers and arithmetic properties; and helping them build a solid foundation and confident dispositions for future mathematics learning. And it is about empowering both teachers and students as mathematical thinkers.

Even those of us who have been doing Number Talks for some time have a lot to learn about how to make them add up to something important—beyond the power in knowing that there are many ways to solve any problem. How do we help students develop flexibility and confidence working with numbers? How can we help each student build a solid foundation for future mathematics learning? What questions do we ask that help students understand important mathematical ideas? What decisions do we make to establish an optimal learning culture in the classroom? How do we best promote a spirit of inquiry and a thirst for knowledge? These questions, and more, are ones that we will grapple with together in this book.

We have not, however, provided step-by-step recipes. Number Talks, if they are to be meaningful, will be organic in nature. While we can plan for each Number Talk by choosing the problem carefully, the discussion about the problem—and where the discussion goes—depends on how our students are thinking.

Before we begin to look at ways to enact Number Talks in classrooms, we examine why this change is needed so you will be prepared for conversations with your colleagues, administrators, parents, and students.

Why Are Number Talks Needed?

Many who have taught middle school or high school mathematics have bemoaned their students' lack of facility with arithmetic. This is nothing new. Decades of research have shown that the traditional curriculum and instructional methods in the United States have left our students with fragile skills and shallow understanding (Hiebert 1999). And every teacher routinely sees students dependent on rote procedures that they apply mindlessly. Unfortunately, examples like this are common:

$$\begin{array}{r} \overset{0}{\cancel{1}}\,\overset{1}{7} \\ -\ 9 \\ \hline 8 \end{array}$$

The work here isn't wrong; the algorithm is done correctly, and the answer is right. Yet, it is a bit disturbing that this student went immediately to the algorithm without first thinking about the problem. Had she done so, she might have realized that following the algorithm would get her nowhere.

Here is another example that we have seen commonly in the middle grades:

$$\frac{1}{3} + \frac{1}{3} = \frac{2}{6} = \frac{1}{3}$$

This student has mixed up rules for fractions. But more disturbing—why didn't this answer raise a red flag that something was amiss? $\frac{1}{3} + \frac{1}{3} = \frac{1}{3}$ makes no sense at all. This brings to mind a memorable observation:

> The depressing thing about arithmetic badly taught is that it destroys a child's intellect, and, to some extent, his integrity. Before they are taught arithmetic, children will not give their assent to utter nonsense; afterwards, they will. (Sawyer 1961)

Teaching arithmetic as a set of rules and procedures to be remembered is the major culprit here. This is not, however, to deny the importance of algorithms. As Hyman Bass points out, arithmetic algorithms are remarkable tools; they are reliable and efficient and they work with all numbers. The trouble is that their very compactness "hides the meaning and complexity of the steps involved" (2003, 323).

Consider, for example, a student's explanation for 63 − 27:

You can't take 7 from 3, so borrow
1 from the 6, and make it a 5.
Put the 1 by the 3, making it a 13.
Now subtract 7 from 13 to get 6.
Then subtract 2 from 5 to get 3.

$$\begin{array}{r} {}^{5}\cancel{6}{}^{1}3 \\ -\ 27 \\ \hline 36 \end{array}$$

The subtraction algorithm conceals the concept of place value in the service of efficiency. Students can get the right answer by treating numbers as columns of *place value–neutral* digits. And, with the value of the digits so far in the background, the relationship between the quantities is lost. The numeral 6 represents 60, but students don't need to know this to get the correct answer. And we can't simply "make the 6 into a 5." It is misleading to let students think that they can "change" numbers. Meanwhile, the idea that 50 + 13 is equal to 63 gets lost in the shuffle.

And another misconception is born here. To help students know when to "borrow," we often say, "You can't take 7 from 3." Actually, you *can* take 7 from 3, and the answer is, of course, −4.

Learning something in second grade and finding out it's not true in seventh grade makes mathematical rules seem arbitrary. We have often had our students ask us, "Are you allowed to . . . ?" as if mathematical procedures are a matter of permission.

Students' fragile understanding of arithmetic follows them into middle school and algebra, where the damage is hard to repair. And, ironically, success in algebra (and beyond) depends on understanding the very concepts that are concealed in algorithms. High school teachers regularly see these kinds of errors:

$$(a+b)^2 = a^2 + b^2$$

$$\frac{x + \cancel{3}}{\cancel{3}} = x$$

We want to be crystal clear here: teachers are not to blame for this sad situation. Most of us only know how to teach mathematics as we have been taught. And even when we try to change our practice, we often have found ourselves caught in a system whose demands run counter to the changes we had wanted to make.

The Standards for Mathematical Practice (NGA/CCSSO 2010) offer a new opportunity. With their focus on "attending to the meaning of quantities, not just how to compute them, and knowing and flexibly using different properties of operations and objects" (SMP2), these standards place mathematical sense-making squarely in the foreground of instruction. Of course, students must be able to compute flexibly, efficiently, and accurately. But they also need to explain their reasoning and determine if the ideas they're using and the results they're getting make sense. And crucially, as Boaler (2008) points out, our students also need to come to believe that these are the things they should always be doing in math class—because this is what mathematics is all about.

Students *do* make sense of computation during Number Talks. For example, here are some of the ways they solved 63 − 27 and the ways we recorded:

I took 30 away from 63 and I got 33. Then I added 3 back on because I took too many away. And 33 + 3 = 36.	I added 3 to 27 to get 30, and then I added 3 to 63 and got 66. And 66 − 30 is 36.

$$63 - 27$$

$$63 - 30 = 33$$
$$\underline{+\ 3}$$
$$36$$

$$63 - 27$$
$$27 + 3 = 30$$
$$63 + 3 = 66$$
$$66 - 30 = 36$$

In contrast to traditional algorithms, Number Talks depend on students' sense-making. Number Talks help students become confident mathematical thinkers more effectively than any single instructional practice we have ever used. There are far too many students who feel like they are no good at math because they aren't quick to get right answers. With Number Talks, students start to believe in themselves mathematically. They become more willing to persevere when solving complex problems. They become more confident when they realize that they have ideas worth listening to. And when students feel this way, the culture of a class can be transformed.

Number Talks are all about students and their ways of thinking. Many teachers, however, don't know how to bring student thinking to the foreground in their classrooms. This book is designed to help you, the teacher, learn to enact Number Talks in ways that help you accomplish this goal.

2

Getting Number Talks Started

Let's get started! The tips and guidance offered here will help you with this rewarding instructional practice, whether you are new to or experienced with Number Talks. Our book doesn't have sequences of problems for you to follow. Instead, there are examples of how and why to choose problems so you can tailor each Number Talk to your own students. And although it might appear that we are suggesting the same kinds of problems over and over again, we aren't. There is a dance between *supporting* and *stretching* students' understanding; its choreography is based on what you learn about your students each time you do a Number Talk. This will become your own formative assessment in action!

The description that follows is as close to a recipe as you will find in this book. Each step in the routine has a rationale. (Note: Most teachers do Number Talks while students are at their regular desks, unless the classroom is large enough to gather students into a half circle, where they can leave their pencils behind and it can be easier to focus.)

1. **Students put paper and pencils away (they may need reminding) and put their fists unobtrusively on their chests to show the teacher they are ready.** This shifts students' attention from working in groups and writing to thinking by themselves.

2. **The teacher writes a problem on the board or document camera.** Generally, we write problems *horizontally* to discourage the use of rote procedures.

3. **The teacher watches while students solve the problem mentally and put up their thumbs when they have had enough time to think.** Giving students whatever time they need is a powerful message about math that challenges the prevalent idea that being good at math means being fast. Also, how quickly—or not—thumbs come up is a good indication of a problem's difficulty. Students who have extra time can be encouraged to solve the problem a second and even third way, and they indicate how many solutions they have by raising that number of fingers silently, so as not to interfere with the thinking of others.

4. **When most thumbs are up, the teacher asks if anyone is willing to share what they think the answer is. She noncommittally records *just the answer* on the board and asks if anyone got a different answer, continuing to record each answer that is given.** Students are asked not to indicate in any way whether they agree or disagree with any given answer; voting on answers has no place in mathematical discourse (see also Chapter 10). You will find that some of the most productive Number Talks occur when students have suggested several different answers.

5. **When the teacher is satisfied there are no other answers, she asks if anyone can explain how he or she figured the problem out.** Describing the steps of a procedure is not enough; students need to be able to explain *why their process makes sense*. There are different ways we ask this question (see below). There is no "right" way, but here are two variations we find ourselves using frequently:
   - *Who has a strategy he or she is willing to share?*
   - *Is anyone willing to convince us that your answer makes sense by telling us what you did?*

6. **When volunteers begin to share their strategies, they first identify which answer (assuming different answers have been offered) they are defending.** Then, as they share their strategies, the teacher records the thinking of each student. (There are many examples of recording in Chapters 4–8.)

7. **After a student shares a strategy, there are several things a teacher might ask in order to work with that student's thinking.** This is the tricky part, and, again, there is no one "right" question. The overall goal is to help the student communicate more clearly and/or to emphasize particular elements of his or her strategy.
   - *Does anyone have a question for _____?*
   - *Can you say more about _____?*

- *Can someone explain _____'s strategy in your own words?*
- *What connections do you notice among the strategies we've discussed?*

As you can see, the Number Talk "routine" is anything but routine. To help you think more about how to respond to students during a discussion, we particularly like Elham Kazemi and Allison Hintz's (2014) *Intentional Talk: How to Structure and Lead Productive Mathematical Discussions.*

8. **Number Talks don't naturally end after fifteen minutes; often, they can go much longer if you let them—and sometimes you may want to let them.** Either way, it's useful to think ahead of time about what you might say to end the Number Talk if there are still students who would like to share their strategies. Usually, we acknowledge that we know some people still have strategies to share and express regret that we don't have more time, and hope that the people who didn't get a chance to share will share tomorrow.

Before You Start

Number Talks turn students' roles in math class upside down. Now they are supposed to figure something out rather than be told the steps to follow. Now they are supposed to explain what *they* think rather than waiting for us to explain. They also are supposed to explain *why*, when in the past knowing *how* was enough. Now they are expected to test new ideas, with mistakes just another part of the process. Now they need to believe that their wrong answers can be opportunities rather than blemishes on their mathematical self-esteem. And the answer isn't what matters most anymore. This is a big change for students.

But it may be an even bigger change for us, as teachers. Helping students develop these dispositions means that *our* roles are turned upside down, too. For those of us—and that's most of us—who were taught that our job is to explain ideas clearly, Number Talks can feel very uncomfortable, especially at first. They may also feel at odds with what we have, in all likelihood, learned that teaching *means*. Teaching as explaining is part of our cultural DNA, so it is natural to wonder how our students will adopt new strategies if we don't first show them to students and explain why they work. Coming to believe that students can—on their own—figure out mathematically valid ways to solve problems can be both liberating and transformative for our teaching.

Number Talks are about students making sense of their own mathematical ideas. The minute we start to explain, we take little bits of their ideas—and their autonomy as thinkers—away. We, in essence, do the thinking for them, robbing them of the emerging and often fragile authority they have over their own reasoning. So we really need to break the habit of *doing the thinking for our students*, if only for these fifteen minutes.

This is a long way of saying that the strategies in the following chapters are not meant to be "taught" in the traditional sense of the word. Rather than giving students a list of strategies to imitate and practice, we try to choose problems that lend themselves to strategies that emerge out of, and build upon, students' existing mathematical understandings. Besides, students don't need to learn every strategy they see. They just need to have strategies that make sense and work efficiently *for them* so that they will be able to reason flexibly with numbers.

Planning the Number Talk

Each Number Talk should have a purpose. Considering where your students are and what strategies they have or have not used will help you think about what they need and how they might approach another problem. We have included a planning template to help you think through what to do and why (see Appendix A: Planning a Number Talk).

Starting Out: Dot Cards

No matter what grade you teach, even high school, so-called "dot" cards (which may not have dots) are a great way to start your students on the path to mathematical reasoning (see Appendix C for a selection of dot card problems). We say this because, from experience, we have realized that with dot cards, students only need to describe what they see—and people have many different ways of seeing! Arithmetic problems, on the other hand, tend to be emotionally loaded for many students. Both of us have found that doing several dot talks before we introduce Number Talks (with numbers) helps establish the following norms:

- There are many ways to see, or do, any problem.
- Everyone is responsible for communicating his or her thinking clearly so that others can understand.
- Everyone is responsible for trying to understand other people's thinking.

To set up the dot talk, tell your students that you are going to show them a card with some shapes on it: "I want you to look at it and, *without counting one by one*, figure out how many [in this case, dots] there are." Remind them to have their fists in a discreet position on their chests and to put up a thumb when they think they know how many dots there are. Then show the dot card; you don't need to leave it up for a few seconds and then hide it. Just leave it up there so students can keep looking at it.

When most thumbs are up, ask who is willing to raise his or her hand and say how many dots are there. Gather the answers—yes, you may get different answers, even in high school!—on the board. Don't write the student's name next to an answer, and don't indicate in any way whether you think an answer is right or wrong. Be sure to double-check: "Who has a different answer?" And wait. Once you have all of the answers, ask who is willing to describe how he or she saw it.

Following is the transcript of the very first Number Talk (for both the students and their teacher) in a high school geometry class. (This is the dot card the teacher used.)

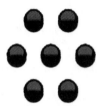

Ms. Phillips:	(Reminds students not to call out the answer.) Okay, I can see almost everyone's thumb. Can I get somebody to tell me how many dots they saw, by raising your hand?
Jorge:	Seven.
Ms. Phillips:	(Records 7 on the board.) Who got a different number? We are sometimes going to get different answers up here, so if you have a different number, please share it.
John:	Eight.
Ms. Phillips:	So we have 7 and 8 . . . any others? Can I have somebody now raise their hand and share how they counted these? Megan?
Megan:	I saw a hexagon that the dots made, and then I counted the one in the middle.
Ms. Phillips:	Megan, first, can you tell us which answer you are defending?
Megan:	Seven.
Ms. Phillips:	Okay, so you saw a hexagon. And how many sides does a hexagon have?
Megan:	Six.
Ms. Phillips:	So, how many dots were on the hexagon?
Megan:	Six, and then I added the one in the middle.
Ms. Phillips:	Did somebody see this differently? Harvey?
Harvey:	I went by twos on the outside. Like, I counted by twos.

Ms. Phillips:	Which is the outside?
Harvey:	The outside of the hexagon.
Ms. Phillips:	So, 2 right here, 2 right here, and 2 right here? And then the middle? So how did you add this in your head?
Harvey:	I did 2 times 3, which equals 6, plus the one dot in the middle.

At this point, Ms. Phillips records Megan's and Harvey's ways of seeing.

Megan ⬠ 6+1

Harvey △ 2×3+1

Ms. Phillips:	(Turns to the class.) Do you see how these are similar, but a little different?
Stephanie:	Megan did the six all at once, but Harvey broke up the six into sections.
Ms. Phillips:	Yeah! Another strategy? Maria?
Maria:	Since it had even sides, I thought of it as a symmetry line. So three on this side, three on that side . . . so three plus three equals six, plus the one in the middle is seven.
Ms. Phillips:	(Represents Maria's thoughts on the board.) Is this how you visualized it?
Maria:	Yeah.
Ms. Phillips:	Where did you see a symmetry line?
Maria:	In the middle.
Ms. Phillips:	(Draws an imaginary vertical line of symmetry on the hexagon with her hand.) Like this?
Maria:	Yeah.
Ms. Phillips:	Another strategy?
Brianna:	I added rows—or columns. I added two plus three plus two.
Ms. Phillips:	Who can see where Brianna might have seen rows of **2 + 3 + 2**?
Stephanie:	Straight across the top, then the middle, then the bottom.

Now, the whiteboard looks like this.

Megan ⬡• 6 + 1   Maria ‹•› 3 + 3 + 1

Harvey △• 2×3+1   Brianna ⚌ 2 + 3 + 2

Ms. Phillips:	Is that right, Brianna? (Brianna nods.) So Brianna saw rows. Would anybody like to defend the 8? (No one volunteers.) How *might* someone think there might be eight dots, do you think?
John:	I saw two parallelograms, so 4 plus 4 is 8. But I forgot that I counted the middle one twice.
Ms. Phillips:	It's awesome that you were willing to share how you thought about your answer even though it was wrong! (Turns to the class.) Many times when we make mistakes, there is a good reason for it, and it can be fun to figure out where we went wrong. Thank you, John. It looks like there were other ways of seeing this, but we are out of time for today. Thank you, everybody, for sharing.

This vignette shows how a dot talk might unfold. While she was teaching, however, Ms. Phillips was juggling competing demands that were invisible to us as we "watched" the Number Talk. She was paying attention to who was sharing, following students' thinking carefully while considering how to record each way of seeing, probing to see how students connected what they "saw" to numbers (for example, Harvey could have been multiplying 2×3 or adding $2 + 2 + 2$), trying hard not to assume that she knew what students were seeing, and thinking about questions she could ask that would help them communicate clearly. She also was probably trying to figure out what to do with John's wrong answer on this very first Number Talk. Along the way, there were many choices she could have made, none of them necessarily "right." This is the challenge—and joy—of *teaching by listening* to students.

Thoughts for Successful Number Talks

After dot cards, there is no "right" place to start Number Talks. Each teacher has different reasons for choosing one operation, or problem, over another. Here, then, are some things for you to think about as you embark on this journey, wherever you choose to begin:

1. ***Being comfortable with plenty of wait time.*** We can't overemphasize the importance of wait time. Students are conditioned to wait for teachers to answer their own questions, so they have a lot more practice at this than their teachers do. We try to wait a *minimum* of ten seconds (practice counting to ten slowly—we did!). Research has shown that there are two different times to wait: after you have asked a question and then again after a student has answered (Rowe 1986). Each time you ask for someone to share in a Number Talk, wait, wait, and then wait some more to give students a chance to gather their thoughts and their courage. And while it may seem that students can outwait you, some of them will become more uncomfortable with the silence than with the thought of sharing their thinking. Sometimes they even laugh at the awkwardness of the silence. That's a good thing. It can get them going. (To learn more about the research supporting wait time, see Mary Budd Rowe's groundbreaking 1987 study "Wait Time: Slowing Down May Be a Way of Speeding Up.")

2. ***Practicing "graduated pressing."*** One of our guiding principles is for teachers to ask questions that encourage students to explain *why* their strategies make sense (see Chapter 3). This kind of questioning is often called "pressing" for conceptual explanations (Kazemi 1998). But students are not used to having a teacher probe their thinking, and explaining clearly is a skill that comes with practice. We have found that pressing too hard when we are getting Number Talks started can be counterproductive. With so little experience, students often have a hard time putting their thoughts into words, and pressing on every single step of a procedure can take so long that it bogs down the Number Talk, leaving no time for other strategies. The other unhappy side effect can be that, until sharing ideas back and forth has become a classroom norm, the thought of being questioned so closely can be intimidating, and thus inhibit class participation. And if students can only think of procedures they have memorized, it's often better *not* to agonize over why those procedures work. In Chapter 10, we share more ideas about how to help students shift from rote thinking to thinking about what makes sense *to them*.

   Dot cards are an exception because students seem to delight in explaining exactly what they see. But arithmetic is emotionally loaded for many students, so when we begin Number Talks with actual numbers, we recommend questioning with a light touch. Saying only what they did—a completely procedural explanation—is still not enough. But in these early Number Talks, one or two questions about why their procedure works are sufficient (see Chapter 5 for a vignette of Mr. Hoffman's class). Then, while "explaining why" is becoming the class norm, we gradually probe more and more deeply, all the while keeping our eye on the goal of creating a class environment in which students are able to make sense, communicate precisely, construct viable arguments, and critique the reasoning of others—the Standards for Mathematical Practices 1, 2, 3, and 6 (NGA/CCSSO 2010).

3. *Thinking together.* When you are just getting started with Number Talks, it is likely that, despite a long wait time, your students have only one way to solve the problem. This is to be expected. Most students have had little experience thinking with numbers, so it is natural that they resort to what they know. And if they have come to believe that there is one right way to solve a problem, they can be reluctant to try something new. If this happens, you might try shifting from asking, "Who thought of it differently?" to asking, "How else could we think about this?"

    The question "How else can we think about this?" turns the Number Talk into a puzzle students try to solve together. Gradually, your students will realize that they can make sense of problems in their own ways and believe that their teacher values different ways over the "right" way.

4. *Learning to listen.* Students will say things that make you think you know what they did or what they saw. But Number Talks are a chance for you to practice genuine curiosity about what students see and to ask questions to make sure you understand what they are saying. Try hard not to jump to conclusions about what they mean or put words in their mouths. When students' explanations are clear, our role is to record what they have said. Other times, though, we may need to rephrase what they have said or ask a probing question to help other students understand the strategy.

5. *Doing Number Talks regularly.* Your students will develop their own mathematical ideas more quickly if you commit to doing a Number Talk every day for two weeks, for example, than if you do those same ten Number Talks over a longer period of time. In order to add up to something mathematically important, Number Talks should build on one another. But when they are spread out to once a week, or even twice a week, students often can't remember ideas or strategies they have seen and so are unable to try them out.

6. ***Encouraging clarity of academic language during students' sharing.*** Students' lack of experience in communicating clearly about mathematics becomes glaringly obvious when they begin to share their thinking during a Number Talk. You will hear a lot of explanations such as "I plussed 4 plus 3," "I timesed 2 and 10," "I minused 5 by 8," or "I added 6 by 7." If students are thinking about mathematics in these ways, it is no wonder that they are stumped when it comes to problems like the following from a typical algebra textbook:

> *One number is 10 more than another. The sum of twice the smaller plus three times the larger is 55. What are the two numbers?*

or

> *The sum of the digits of a certain two-digit number is 7. Reversing its digits increases the number by 9. What is the number?*

We have found that students' use of mathematical language improves gradually, over time, through Number Talks. This is also true for English learners. Participation in mathematical discussions, such as those that occur during Number Talks where genuine student contributions and interactions are integral, has been shown to be important for language learners. The work of Judit Moschkovich (1999) has been instrumental in helping us understand how and why Number Talks are important for English language learners. At first, the most important goal must be to get students' ideas in the public thinking space and tread gently on the language they use. She cautions against some currently popular practices that sound good in theory but in reality serve to limit language acquisition, such as attending more closely to vocabulary and pronunciation than on getting students' ideas on the table.

7. ***Recording thinking.*** Recording is a way of representing clearly to the whole class how the student was thinking. It also gives us a chance to model correct notation and ask questions along the way. For these reasons, we don't have students come to the board to record their strategies. We also don't recommend the use of individual white boards or iPads because students are much more likely to fall back on rote methods.

There is no "right way" to record students' thinking. Any method can be recorded in a variety of ways, and the most important thing to consider is how best to make a student's ideas clear to the rest of the class. Figuring out how to do this will sometimes be challenging, and you might fumble at times. And there is often a tension between recording what students say and wanting them to recognize more formal mathematical notation. But don't be in a hurry to use algebraic notation. Symbols have no inherent meaning in and of themselves. They have meaning only when students understand the relationships they represent, and you are the best judge of when to connect what students already understand to symbolic notation. Deciding what to write—and how—is both a judgment call and an art, and you will get better over time, just as students will get better at expressing their ideas.

The many examples of recordings throughout this book have a purposeful lack of consistency. Sometimes, for example, we use × to represent multiplication (to ease the abstraction) and other times we use other symbols; sometimes we use parentheses and other times we don't. We have done this to encourage you to try different things—as long as they are mathematically accurate, of course—and find ways that are best for your students. Ultimately, we want students to work flexibly both with mathematical ideas and their symbolic representations.

8. ***Trying to get students to talk to one another without going through you.*** Physically positioning yourself to the side of the room helps get you out of the spotlight (even though you are pretty much tethered there as a recorder of student thinking). After a student explains a strategy, wait to give space for another student to speak (instead of you). If hands go up, rather than calling on students yourself, have the person presenting the idea call on the students.

9. ***Making the most of multiple answers.*** Multiple answers to the same problem offer wonderful opportunities to learn. When there are multiple answers, we sometimes find ourselves saying, "Great! I'm not saying *great* because some of you got wrong answers. I'm saying great because now you have a chance to do what mathematicians often have to do: convince skeptics. And we have skeptics in the room now, so who would like to convince us that your answer makes sense?"

But what about wrong answers? While some wrong answers come from little mistakes, as with John's mistake, others have logic that, if explored, gives everyone a chance to learn something new.

A Wrong Answer to Learn From

Ms. Yu has just posed the problem 28 × 12. After a few strategies have been shared, Elisa raises her hand.

Elisa: Uh, I did something different, but I got the wrong answer, and I don't know what I did wrong.

Ms. Yu: Cool! So what did you get the first time?

Elisa: Uh, 132. But I already knew it was wrong because looking at those numbers, it can't possibly be 132.

Ms. Yu: Why can't it be 132?

Elisa: Because 12 times 12 is 144, and 12 times 28 has to be bigger.

Ms. Yu: So, can you walk us through how you did it?

Elisa: I knew 7 times 4 is 28, so I did 7 × 12 and then 4 × 12. And then I added them and got 132.

Here's how Ms. Yu recorded Elisa's strategy. Can you figure out Elisa's mistake?

$$28 \times 12$$
$$(7 \times 4) \times 12$$
$$7 \times 12 = 84$$
$$4 \times 12 = 48$$
$$84 + 48 = 132$$

Ms. Yu: Elisa used this really great reasoning to know that her answer is wrong. Can somebody figure out what Elisa did and where she might have gone wrong? Talk to someone near you about what you think happened.

Elisa had thought about the problem as (7 × 4) × 12, but she used the distributive property as if there were an addition sign instead of a multiplication sign between 7 and 4. This is a common mistake. Examining Elisa's error gave the whole class an opportunity to learn—not only about the associative and distributive properties but also about how important and useful mistakes can be.

10. ***Helping students learn to express themselves more clearly.*** Most of our students have had so little experience expressing themselves clearly that they need a lot of help and practice. But if students are not able to express their ideas clearly, their peers won't be able to understand them, which results in fewer opportunities for students to comment directly to one another. We have found that the following strategies help facilitate clear student expression:

   - Encourage students to speak loudly enough so everyone can hear.
   - Remind students about why clearly communicating their thinking is so important.
   - Discourage (or ban) the use of pronouns like *it* ("I multiplied *it* by 5"), and press students to clarify what they mean by *it*. Cathy and her colleagues put this sign up in their classrooms:

$$\varnothing\ it$$

11. ***Having a backup plan in place.*** If students take a very long time to put up their thumbs, it could be that the problem you have chosen is too hard—or too easy—for them to want to engage in. One of our colleagues always has two backup problems ready so she isn't caught trying to make up a new problem on the fly.

12. ***Knowing when it's okay to share your way of thinking during Number Talks.*** There are times when our students are so stuck in one way of thinking that we feel like we have to do something. There may be a new method that we've discovered or a strategy that we know of that is both efficient and mathematically interesting—a strategy we aren't hearing from our students. In these circumstances, we might tell students we want to share how we thought about the problem or that we want to show them something we have seen other kids do. But our students are so susceptible to the power of our statements, and their belief in their own thinking is so fragile, that we have to be very, very careful when we suggest things in class.

   Once your students love Number Talks—and they will!—you will become part of the learning community. It is okay to try out new ideas and share your own discoveries with students. You'll want to be sure to share honestly with them when you're confused about an idea or strategy. It is actually a gift to students when we are able to do this, and it models behaviors that we hope to see from them. When you share an idea or strategy, just be sure that you are first listening to students, that you have become an authentic part of the learning community, and that you are not conveying in any way that you value your own strategy over theirs.

13. **"Nudging" students to move beyond traditional algorithms.** Middle and high school students often come to math class with a host of memorized procedures but little experience in making sense of the operations. In fact, most have come to believe being good at math means that you can add, subtract, multiply, and divide quickly *without* thinking. When students are taught arithmetic by following procedures, the underlying mathematical relationships are generally not understood. So asking them to suddenly understand *why*, when always before it was enough to know *how*, can seem baffling (see Chapter 10 for more ideas to help students move beyond rote thinking). Following is an example of how we sometimes introduce Number Talks to high school students:

> We know you have learned a lot of ways to do math over the years, but today we are going to try something new. We are going to give you problems to do that you may have learned how to do a long time ago. But this time, we want you to try to do them in your head using a way that makes the problem easy for you to figure out.

Please don't worry if you haven't internalized all of these suggestions when you begin Number Talks. When we first started, we really had no idea what we were doing. We just knew that our students had such a fragile understanding of numbers that we needed to try something new. You and your students will find your way together. What's most important is that you commit to embarking on this journey.

3

Guiding Principles for Enacting Number Talks in the Classroom

Daily experience with Number Talks can, over time, help students build competence, flexibility, and confidence as mathematical thinkers. But this does not happen automatically. The power of Number Talks emerges only when our teaching practices support students in making sense of the mathematics *for themselves*. There are reasons to intervene, or not; reasons to give answers, or not; reasons to probe, or not. Helping students make sense of mathematical ideas through Number Talks requires instructional decisions that are purposeful and yet may run counter to what we traditionally think of as "teaching."

In this chapter, we offer some principles for working with students of all ages that guide our decision making as we implement Number Talks in our classrooms. We've come to think of these as our "Guiding Principles for Number Talks." (We are indebted to Kathy Richardson, whose Guiding Principles in California State Department of Education's (1988) *Mathematics Model Curriculum Guide: Kindergarten Through Grade Eight* have inspired and grounded our teaching for many years.) We hope these "Guiding Principles" will become foundational for your teaching decisions as you help students build powerful understandings and come to believe in themselves as mathematical thinkers through engaging in Number Talks.

Guiding Principles for Number Talks

1. All students have mathematical ideas worth listening to, and our job as teachers is to help students learn to develop and express these ideas clearly.

Students need opportunities to think and learn to solve problems in ways that make sense to them. In Number Talks, as students listen to other students' strategies, and as they look for relationships among different solutions, their mathematical understanding is deepened. It is through the investigation of the diverse ways of seeing and solving problems that students develop a robust understanding of mathematics.

2. Through our questions, we seek to understand students' thinking.

Our questions matter. Questions can open up mathematical discourse, or they can close it down by "funneling" students' thinking in a particular direction. Questions that encourage discourse express our genuine curiosity about how students are thinking. They require students to articulate and express, and thereby better understand, their own and one another's ideas. "What were you thinking when you . . . ?" or "Why did you divide by ten?" are often called *authentic* questions. While we may have a good idea about how students are thinking, we don't *really* know until we ask. Authentic questions keep the mathematical focus where it belongs: on students' reasoning—not ours.

In order to keep students' ideas at the forefront, however, we need to listen closely to what they are saying. Listening carefully *to* students—rather than listening *for* what we hope to hear—is essential for productive Number Talks. Listening "to" helps us know what questions to ask next and what directions to take with a student's ideas.

It is far too easy, however, to unconsciously direct students' thinking through our questions. Questions that end in "right?" (for example, "You took away thirty, so you had to put two back, right?") are examples of explanations "in disguise" that tend to replace children's thinking with our own. It is understandable to want students to express ideas the way we understand them or to be able to use a method that we think is easiest. But when our goal is to teach students that they have mathematical ideas worth listening to, it is important that our questions focus on helping them make sense of the mathematics in their own ways so that they learn to express their ideas with confidence and competence.

3. We encourage students to explain their thinking conceptually rather than procedurally.

It is not enough for students to know what they did to solve a problem. In today's world, knowing what to do is no longer sufficient. Our students must understand and be able to explain *why* their procedures make sense (see Standards for Mathematical Practice 1 and 2 [NGA/ CCSSO 2010]). Making a habit of asking "Why did you . . . ?" questions can help students dig deeper into a problem in order to understand why their procedures or strategies will or will not work. These questions will also help students eventually begin to ask those questions of themselves and one another.

When students are new to Number Talks, we have found that most of them will use only traditional algorithms because that is what they have learned. When they try to explain their strategy, though, their explanations are nearly always procedural. And while it still is important to ask "Why?" in these moments, spending too much time probing for the meaning of procedures that students have simply memorized can be counterproductive and discouraging. Many students don't know why algorithms work—and never have been expected to know why—so it is a bit unfair to ask. Students will soon realize that the traditional algorithms become unwieldy as the numbers get larger. It is okay to acknowledge this and suggest that they might want to look for more efficient ways to compute mentally.

4. Mistakes provide opportunities to look at ideas that might not otherwise be considered.

Mistakes are necessary for learning. It is not enough to say that mistakes are "celebrated." The collective examination and understanding of mistakes as a regular part of mathematics instruction can shift students' erroneous views of mathematics-as-answer-getting and help them learn to analyze the validity of procedures. Many mistakes involve conceptual errors that, if closely examined, focus students' attention on the structure of problems and the properties that underlie mathematical operations. In this way, mistakes can be valuable sites for learning (Hiebert et al. 1997).

As recent brain research has shown, the examination of mistakes sparks a firing of synapses and growth in neurons that cause the brain to grow. In *Mindset: The New Psychology of Success,* Carol Dweck (2006) addresses the importance of nurturing a "growth mindset" in students. Students with a growth mindset view mistakes as opportunities to learn something new, while those with a "fixed mindset" tend to see mistakes as something to avoid and cover up. Students who see mistakes as an important part of learning are more likely to persevere.

5. While efficiency is a goal, we recognize that whether or not a strategy is efficient lies in the thinking and understanding of each individual learner.

No strategy is efficient for a student who does not yet understand it. Number Talks are not about getting our students to think like we do, or even to get them to understand a "best" way. Rather, they are about encouraging students to think in ways that make sense *to them*.

Occasionally it is okay, or even important, to "shine a light" on a particularly efficient and generalizable idea or to ask students to try another student's method, but it is important that we do so in ways that do not convey to students that this is a strategy we favor or expect them to remember. Similarly, asking students to judge one another's methods or identify those strategies that are most efficient can also be discouraging—and even counterproductive—particularly to a student who has just tried out a new idea that may not prove to be very efficient.

We don't mean to imply that efficiency is not important. Together with accuracy and flexibility, efficiency is a hallmark of numerical fluency. And it is undeniable that some strategies are more efficient than others. (See Chapters 4 through 8 for ways to nudge students in the direction of greater flexibility and efficiency.)

6. We seek to create a learning environment where all students feel safe sharing their mathematical ideas.

Not every student needs to—or should be expected to—talk in every setting. Our goal is to help all students feel safe enough during Number Talks that they are willing to share their ways of seeing and solving problems. There are many reasons, however, why students may not want to share during a classroom discussion: lack of confidence in their ability to speak English or in their mathematical reasoning, or even overall shyness. If we want a safe learning environment where students will become comfortable testing out their mathematical ideas, then they must be in control of whether (and when) they share an idea publicly.

We are aware that this principle runs counter to current accountability practices such as "equity" sticks or cold-calling. But researchers in psychology have found that stress interferes with performance in mathematics problem-solving tasks by reducing the working memory capacity (Beilock 2011). Knowing that they must be ready to speak at any time, whether they want to or not, can interfere with students' learning. Therefore, we need to be purposeful about finding ways to encourage all students to share their thinking without putting them on the spot or pressuring them. Our job is to make Number Talks a safe place for students to try out new ideas and to share their thinking when they are ready to do so.

7. One of our most important goals is to help students develop social and mathematical agency.

Students with a sense of agency recognize that they are an important part of an intellectual community in the classroom; that they have worthwhile ideas to contribute, and that they learn from considering, and building on, the ideas of others. They know that they have choices, and they take responsibility for the choices they make. They have a disposition to take action as a learner: they can defend their ideas when asked to and change their mind only when convinced by reason. When it comes to mathematics, their identity is that of a mathematical thinker. They persevere at solving problems, and they are not satisfied until something makes sense. They look to the reasonableness of the mathematics, and not to the teacher or others, to determine whether an idea is sound.

To help students develop a sense of agency, we need to learn to make decisions that help take us out of the focal center of the classroom by sharing authority for classroom discourse with students. This also means recognizing and encouraging any sign of student agency as it arises in the classroom—the very first time, for example, that a student responds directly to another student during a mathematics discussion. And, because praise tends to keep students dependent on us, we need to be extremely careful about how and what we praise.

8. Mathematical understandings develop over time.

Encountering a mathematical idea multiple times in a variety of contexts is necessary for real understanding. Students come to us with well-developed notions about what it means to do mathematics, and most have rarely been asked to make sense of numbers in their own ways. Number Talks often uncover a lack of foundational knowledge that has been hidden by the practice of procedures, so students need plenty of time to rebuild what they have lost. They may need to test out a mathematical idea many times before being able to apply and explain the idea fluently, or they may need to try on an idea that they hear from someone else several times before they own the idea themselves.

For the same reasons, it may take some students quite a while before they come to see the value in Number Talks. Some students will need to learn to value the process before they really invest themselves in the thinking required by Number Talks. While we know this isn't a *mathematical* understanding, it involves beliefs and attitudes about what mathematics is and how students see their role in their mathematics classes. For older students, these beliefs have developed over a long period of time, so as teachers, we need to have faith in the process and perseverance in the face of periodic discouragement.

9. Confusion and struggle are natural, necessary, and even desirable parts of learning mathematics.

We need to be careful not to put confusion—that process of being in cognitive dissonance or of not knowing—to rest prematurely. Rather than avoiding it, both teachers and students can learn to embrace confusion, knowing that it can be the beginning of new understandings. But when teachers are too quick to put students' cognitive dissonance to rest, students miss out on the chance to struggle with ideas—a necessity in learning mathematics. This may mean redefining for ourselves what it means to "help" students. Rather than protecting them from confusion, we need to help students by encouraging their willingness to struggle and their perseverance.

However, not all confusion is a good thing. We need to clear up confusion if we have posed a problem poorly or if students are missing information they need. But when the confusion involves mathematical relationships, or what Piaget calls "logico-mathematical knowledge" (Labinowicz 1980), we need to help students learn to honor the struggle as they strive to solve a problem or make sense of a mathematical idea. Ideally, we want them to learn to embrace confusion, or disequilibrium, recognizing it as an indication that they are likely at the threshold of learning something new.

It is uncomfortable and downright hard, though, not to help students when they are confused. As teachers, we have been taught to help students by explaining procedures clearly, so the idea of letting students grapple with uncertainty goes against what most of us have learned that teaching *is*. And students have become so used to this kind of help that they often give up or don't bother trying to figure things out; instead, they simply wait for us to bail them out.

This was made blatantly clear to Stacey, a high school Algebra 2 teacher, when she asked her students, "How do you feel when you try to solve a problem you haven't seen before?" The following direct quotes are typical of her students' responses:

Jamie: Very uncertain because I think I could be using the wrong kind of equation or way of solving it.

Alex: When I see a problem that I don't know, I don't attempt it at all because I want to see an example of it first before I try because I don't want to be wrong.

Alicia: I feel like giving up when I don't already know how to do it because I rely on my teacher to explain it.

We have all seen students who have given up on math and students who ask us to just tell them what to do. We have to remember, though, that this is learned behavior. But to be successful in life, students need to be willing to approach problems they've never seen before. And it will take work on our part, and feelings of success on their part, for students to build new beliefs about themselves and mathematics.

10. We value and encourage a diversity of ideas.

Through Number Talks, students develop a disposition to listen to and build on the ideas of their peers and teachers. Students need to work with numbers flexibly, efficiently, and accurately, and coming to understand the varied ways that problems can be solved is essential for both students and teachers.

Students need to know that no matter the problem, people won't all see or solve it in the same way. And we want them to learn that when they listen to and build on one another's ideas, and look for relationships among our diverse ways of seeing, everyone learns more deeply and understands more clearly. As Ruth has said on many occasions, "I've come to believe that my job is *not* to teach my students to see what I see. My job is to teach them to see."

We hope these "Guiding Principles for Number Talks" will help you in moment-by-moment decision making as you enact Number Talks in your classroom. We know, from experience, that the payoff will be huge. As students learn together that there are multiple ways to solve problems, and as they learn that they can make sense of mathematics in their own ways, mathematical discourse in the classroom is enhanced. Students find themselves regularly using the Standards for Mathematical Practice: learning to reason mathematically, making mathematically convincing arguments, and critiquing the reasoning of others (NGA/CCS-SO 2010). They come to know that cognitive dissonance is a good thing. And most of all, students come to believe that mathematics makes sense and that they have mathematical ideas worth listening to.

Prelude to the Operations

Concentrating on one arithmetic operation at a time gives students many opportunities to try out strategies that they haven't seen before and to think deeply and flexibly about the operation. Only you, however, can decide which operation is the most appropriate starting place for your students. Therefore, Chapters 4 through 7 can be done in any order. They have the same general structure that will make this book easy to use, no matter where you choose to start. We also include here three kinds of Number Talks that don't fit in any one chapter; rather, they help students use several strategies across the operations with ease. Finally, we have a special note for those of you who teach high school.

How the Chapters Are Organized

For each operation, we—
- highlight and informally name four or five of the most efficient strategies;
- discuss how each strategy works and how it supports mathematical understanding;
- show an example of how a student might describe the strategy;
- give examples of how you might record students' thinking;
- list sample problems to get you started, along with suggestions on how to encourage students' use of the strategy;
- offer ideas for increasingly challenging problems, including fractions, decimals, and integers; and
- include, from time to time, vignettes from actual classroom interactions to give you a better sense of how a Number Talk might evolve.

We want to stress that the strategies are not a list of "things to teach"; we include them to help you anticipate the kinds of strategies that students often use. Besides, students frequently have a difficult time explaining what they did, so the more ways *you* can think about it, the more easily you will be able to ask questions to help students articulate their thinking clearly.

And don't forget that it's not important for each student to use every strategy! The important thing is that students have at least one strategy that they understand and have made sense of. While it is true that having a variety of strategies can help students reason more flexibly with numbers, students who are required to use strategies they don't understand might as well be using traditional algorithms. That said, there are times when we hope students will try out a new method, and we may nudge them in a particular direction. No matter how carefully you might choose a problem that you think will certainly elicit a particular strategy, though, it's possible that no one will think to use it. Don't worry about this—it means students aren't ready to use that strategy . . . yet.

Three Basics for Number Talks

Three special cases of arithmetic operations, which we call the "basics," can be interspersed throughout your usual Number Talks. These special cases can help students reason more easily with numbers across operations. For each, we will use the number 36 as an example. As with all Number Talks, in each of these cases teacher questioning is important to flesh out a student's reasoning.

1. **Doubling Any Number (a special case of addition or multiplication)**
    Middle grades are the time when students transition from additive to multiplicative thinking. When doubling, students often use both, so it is good to draw explicit connections between them.

    To begin, tell students that you are going to write a number on the board and you want them to double it. Write *Double 36* on the board. When most thumbs are up, proceed with the Number Talk structure: collecting answers, asking for explanations, and so on. Ways your students might think about this include:

    > "I added thirty and thirty and got sixty; then I added six and six and got twelve. Sixty and twelve is seventy-two."
    >
    > "I multiplied two times thirty and got sixty; then I multiplied two times six and got twelve. Sixty and twelve is seventy-two."
    >
    > "I doubled thirty-five instead because I knew that two times thirty-five is seventy. And then I just added two more to get seventy-two."
    >
    > "I knew four times nine is thirty-six so I just did eight times nine and got seventy-two."

    Don't be surprised if some students don't know what it means to double a number.

2. **Halving Any Number (special case of division)**

    Tell students that you are going to write a number on the board and you want them to let you know with their thumbs when they know what half of the number is. Write *36* on the board and proceed as you did with doubling. Ways your students might think about this include:

    > "I knew that fifteen plus fifteen is thirty, so half of thirty is fifteen. And then three plus three is six, so fifteen plus three is eighteen."
    >
    > "I divided thirty by two and got fifteen; then I divided six by two and got three. So fifteen plus three equals eighteen."
    >
    > "I knew eighteen and eighteen makes thirty-six."

    Don't rush to use large numbers. It helps students to become fluent with halving single-digit numbers and numbers to twenty before tackling larger numbers.

3. **Getting from Any Number to the Next Larger Power of Ten**

    Tell students you are going to write a number on the board and you want them to let you know when they know what to add to get to one hundred (or one thousand, and so on). Write *36* on the board. Ways your students might think about this include:

    > "I added four to get to forty and then sixty to get to one hundred. So altogether, sixty-four."
    >
    > "I added sixty to thirty-six and got ninety-six; and then I only needed four more to get to one hundred."
    >
    > "I thought about one hundred as ninety and ten. So I knew thirty and sixty is ninety, and four and six is ten, so I need thirty-four."

    When we've had Number Talks about getting to the next larger power of ten like the above with students, we haven't even recorded their ideas. We're not sure whether that was a good idea or not, but our emphasis was on helping students learn to begin talking about numbers and their thinking with ease. We did several Number Talks in a row, and it just took a few minutes of practice until thumbs were coming up quickly. If students practice Number Talks often enough, they can get from any number, no matter how large or small, to the next power of ten, fairly comfortably.

Arithmetic in High School?

Many high school teachers—and possibly their students—are concerned when Number Talks don't seem to be dealing with so-called high school content. We have learned not to worry about this, even knowing full well that there isn't enough time to teach everything in our courses anyway.

This is because students' ability to reason with numbers is the bedrock of their understanding of algebra and therefore is in everyone's curriculum. Number Talks offer your students the opportunity to communicate and justify their thinking—a mathematical practice with which they sorely need experience.

There is a lot of rational number arithmetic that arises during algebra, geometry, and beyond, and any time numbers are involved in a formula, expression, or equation, there is an opportunity to do a Number Talk that fits your curriculum. However, it's important to be alert for opportunities as they arise. Geometry, in particular, is rich with potential because of the many ways to approach each problem:

- finding the volume of a prism
- finding the perimeter of irregular figures
- figuring out the radius of a circle when given the diameter or vice versa
- finding the measure of complementary and supplementary angles
- figuring out the measure of the third angle of a triangle when given the measures of two angles
- figuring out the area of a sector of a circle when given the measure of the central angle of the sector and the area of the circle
- finding the area of a rectangle, parallelogram, or triangle when given the base and height
- approximating the area of a circle when given the radius
- finding the measure of an angle in degrees when given its measure in radians—for example, $13\pi/8$

We are sure that you will think of additional ways to weave Number Talks into your high school mathematics classes!

4 | Subtraction Across the Grades

We chose to focus first on subtraction for a couple of reasons. It is an appropriate operation to begin with when introducing older students to Number Talks. Middle and high school students sometimes think that addition problems are "too easy." Also, students typically find subtraction challenging (even though we teach it every year from first grade on), and they are often happy to learn that they can solve subtraction problems in ways that make sense to them.

There are two main meanings of subtraction: subtraction as taking away (removing) and subtraction as the difference, or distance, between two numbers. By the time they reach fourth grade, however, students usually think about subtraction as "take away." Understanding subtraction as distance is often overlooked despite its importance. In algebra, geometry, and calculus, students use formulas—for the slope of a line, the distance formula, or for finding the area under a curve—in which subtraction indicates the length of a line segment. (For a thorough discussion of the importance and uses of subtraction as distance in higher mathematics, see Harris 2011.) Therefore, in this chapter we focus on helping students develop an intuitive understanding of subtraction as distance. When students have experienced these concepts through Number Talks, they will have a solid foundation for the mathematics to come.

We use $63 - 28$ as a sample problem to demonstrate five subtraction strategies that work efficiently across the continuum of rational numbers—that is, from whole numbers through fractions, decimals, and percents. Even though some of these strategies might be new to you, resist "teaching" them because students often come up with these strategies on their own.

> ### A Note About Recording: The Open Number Line
>
> As you'll see, we often use an "open number line" as a recording strategy during Number Talks to give students a visual model for their thinking.
>
> Open number lines have no scale and thus are not meant to be accurate measures of units. Rather, the "jumps" can be roughly proportional. A nice thing about the open number line is it allows for really large or small numbers without having to worry about individual units.

Five Strategies for Subtraction

> Minuend − Subtrahend = Difference

63 − 28

1. Round the Subtrahend to a Multiple of Ten and Adjust:

"I rounded 28 to 30. Then I subtracted 30 from 63 and got 33. Then I added 2 back because I had taken away 2 too many."

$$63 - 28$$
$$63 - 30 = 33$$
$$\frac{+\ 2}{35}$$

2. Decompose the Subtrahend:

"First I took 20 from 63 and that was 43. Then, I saw the 8 in 28 as a 3 and 5; I took away the 3 from 43 first and that was 40; then I took away the 5 and that was 35."

$$63 - 28$$
$$63 - 20 = 43$$
$$\frac{-\ 3}{40}$$
$$\frac{-\ 5}{35}$$

3. Add Instead:

There are several ways a student might get from 28 to 63 by adding.

Way 1: First, get to a multiple of 10: "I started with 28 and added 2 to get 30; then I added 33 and got 63. So altogether I added 2 and 33, or 35."

$$63 - 28$$

$$28 + 2 = 30$$
$$+ 33$$
$$\overline{63}$$

or

$$63 - 28$$

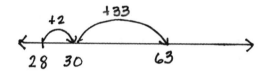

Way 2: First, get to a multiple of 10, and then add a multiple of 10: "I started at 28 and added 2 to get to 30. Then I added 30 to get to 60, and then I added 3 to get to 63. I added 2 plus 30 plus 3 to get 35 as my answer."

$$63 - 28$$

$$28 \widehat{(+\,2)} = 30$$
$$\widehat{(+\,30)}$$
$$60 \widehat{(+\,3)} = 63$$

$$2 + 30 + 3 = 35$$

or

$$63 - 28$$

Way 3: First, add a multiple of 10: "I started at 28 and jumped 30 to get to 58. Then I jumped 2 more to get to 60 and 3 more to get to 63. Altogether I jumped 35."

$$63 - 28$$

$$28 \widehat{+ 30} = 58$$
$$\widehat{+ 2}$$
$$60 \widehat{+ 3} = 63$$

$$30 + 2 + 3 = 35$$

or

63-28

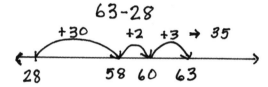

28   58 60 63

4. Same Difference:

"I added 2 to 28 and got 30; then I added 2 to 63 and got 65. And 65 minus 30 is 35."

$$+2 \Big(\begin{array}{c} 63 - 28 \\ 65 - 30 \end{array} \Big) +2$$

$$35$$

or

$$63 - 28$$
$$65 - 30 = 28$$

30   65
+2   +2
28   63

5. Break Apart by Place:

"60 minus 20 is 40; 3 minus 8 is negative 5; 40 minus 5 is 35."

$$63 - 28$$

$$\begin{array}{r} 63 \\ -\ 28 \\ \hline 40-5 \\ 35 \end{array}$$

Developing the Subtraction Strategies in Depth

1. Round the Subtrahend to a Multiple of Ten:

Rounding the subtrahend can be useful for the removal or "take-away" meaning of subtraction. To encourage the use of this strategy, we purposely select problems with a subtrahend (the number that is taken away) that is close to a multiple of ten, one hundred, and so on, so that it "cries out" to be rounded. Taking away a multiple of ten, and then compensating/adjusting, makes subtraction easier while still maintaining the sense of quantity. This strategy is particularly useful when students hang on to the traditional algorithm and need to be coaxed to try something easier.

How to choose problems that invite students to Round the Subtrahend:

We usually start with a few problems that subtract 8s or 9s from a two-digit number, such as:

$$13 - 9 \qquad 24 - 8 \qquad 61 - 8 \qquad 43 - 9$$

Sometimes we find that students more readily use this strategy for two-digit subtrahends that are close to a multiple of 10, such as:

$$63 - 28 \qquad 71 - 39 \qquad 84 - 59 \qquad 42 - 19 \qquad 50 - 28$$

Then with a three-digit number minus a two-digit number, we look for two-digit numbers that are close to 100 so that the strategy makes the problem easier and more efficient:

$$134 - 99 \qquad 247 - 98 \qquad 315 - 97 \qquad 468 - 99$$

Gradually, you can move the subtrahend farther and farther away from a target multiple—for example, $54 - 28$ or $81 - 17$. The type of problem you choose will depend on the cognitive maturity and/or experience of your students.

Questions that are useful for the strategy of Rounding the Subtrahend:

- Why did you take [200] away instead of [198]?
- Did you take away too many or too few?
- Why did you add [2] twice?

This last question, "Why did you add twice?," can reveal soft spots in a student's thinking. Consider the brief vignette below from a fifth-grade classroom:

Ms. Young writes the problem 43 − 28 on the board and waits for students to raise their thumbs, indicating that they have figured out the answer.

Ms. Young:	Is anyone willing to share the answer you got?
Tim:	15.
Ms. Young:	Did anyone get a different answer that you would be willing to share?
Jennifer:	I got 11.
Ms. Young:	Does anyone have a different answer? (No one does.)
Ms. Young:	Is anyone willing to try to convince us that you have an answer that makes sense?
Jason:	I'm defending 15. 28 was hard for me to think about, so I took 30 away from 43 and that gave me 13. But I took away too much so I added 2 back on and I got 15.
Ms. Young:	Why did you add 2?
Jason:	When I took away 30, I took away 2 too much, so I had to put 2 back on.
Ms. Young:	Thank you for getting us started, Jason. Did anyone think about it differently?
Angel:	I did. I got 15, too, but I started with 28 and added up. I added 2 to get to 30, and then I added 13 to get to 43. So altogether I added 15.
Ms. Young:	Does anyone have a question for Angel? (No one does.) Did anyone think about it a different way?
Jennifer:	I know my answer is wrong, but I can't figure out why.
Ms. Young:	Do you want to share what you did? (Jennifer nods.)
Jennifer:	I did it like Jason. I took 30 away from 43 and that was 13. Since I added 2 to 28, I took the 2 away from 13 and I got 11.

Ms. Young:	Why did you add the 2?
Jennifer:	I added it to 28 because 30 was easier to take away.
Ms. Young:	So when you took away 30, did you take away too many or too few?
Jennifer:	I took away too many.
Ms. Young:	You took away too many. So will you have to take away more, or will you have to put some back?

Ms. Young hoped her questions would help focus Jennifer on the action she had taken so she would know how to compensate for the change she had made. At another time she might have asked the class to try to figure out what Jennifer had done, but Ms. Young was hoping to squeeze in a quick Number Talk this day, and she was sure that this particular confusion would surface again when she would hopefully have more time to let other students talk about this.

| **Jennifer:** | Well . . . I have to take away what I added. . . . Oh, wait. No. Now I see what I did wrong. When I took away 30, I took off 2 too many, so I have to add them back. So now I agree with 15. |

Ms. Young tucks this away to come back to another day. She knows that this idea can be counterintuitive for students and that very interesting and mathematically important discussions might ensue.

Rounding the Subtrahend with Fractions and Decimals

Rounding the subtrahend works with decimals much like it does with whole numbers. We choose subtrahends that can easily be rounded to a whole number. When there are a different number of decimal places in the subtrahend, students have a little more to think about.

Decimals Example: $4.34 - 1.97$

$$4.34 - 1.97$$

$$4.34 - 2 = 2.34$$
$$+.03$$
$$\overline{2.37}$$

"I rounded 1.97 to 2; then I subtracted 2 from 4.34 and that gave me 2.34. Then I had to add .03 back because I took away too many. So I got 2.37."

Problems to get you started:

$3.63 - 1.95$ **$3.6 - 1.95$**   **$3.63 - 1.9$**

Fractions work the same way, although they may seem harder because of the weak understanding of fractions that some students have. Again, we want to use a subtrahend close to a whole number. We start with denominators in which one is a factor of the other. Fourths and eighths are a good place to start. Here are some examples to get you started.

$3\frac{1}{4} - 1\frac{7}{8}$ **$6\frac{1}{8} - 2\frac{5}{8}$**   **$3\frac{1}{2} - 1\frac{5}{6}$**

2. Decompose the Subtrahend:

Decompose (or break up) the Subtrahend is a "removal" strategy that students often take up before other strategies. This is an important strategy because students learn that they can take numbers apart in order to reason in more efficient ways.

Decompose the Subtrahend uses students' comfort with subtracting multiples of ten and their fluency with small numbers. Decomposing the subtrahend can give students confidence as they are learning to use strategies that make sense to them.

How to choose problems that invite Decompose the Subtrahend:

Decomposing the subtrahend is a strategy that students use naturally. In order to encourage this strategy, we start with two-digit-minus-one-digit problems where the subtrahend is larger than the ones digit in the minuend and not too close to 10.

Problems to get you started:

$32 - 6$ **$21 - 8$**   **$13 - 7$**   **$43 - 7$**   **$44 - 8$**   **$61 - 7$**

Once students have begun to use this strategy, they will apply it to larger problems such as:

$$43 - 17 \qquad 62 - 16 \qquad 47 - 28 \qquad 83 - 37 \qquad 91 - 26 \qquad 84 - 36$$

Unfortunately, this strategy pretty quickly becomes less efficient as the numbers get larger. But using it gives students easy access to thinking about subtraction in new ways and thus makes sense as an early focus in Number Talks. Don't worry about this. You'll find that students will gravitate to strategies that work more efficiently with a broad range of problems.

Questions that are useful for Decompose the Subtrahend:
- How did you decide what to take away?
- Why did you want to break the numbers apart?
- Did anyone break the subtrahend apart in a different way?

3. Add Instead:

Adding to subtract is an efficient way to do problems that don't work so easily by rounding the subtrahend. The idea that they might never have to subtract again delights many students. And, when recording on an open number line, this strategy also sets the stage for understanding subtraction as the distance between two numbers.

How to choose problems that invite students to Add Instead:

When students see two numbers that are close together, someone will usually find the difference by adding up. When recording, it is important to make sure students know where the answer is (see pages 39 and 40).

When choosing problems for this strategy, we look for subtrahends that are much like those that we chose for Round the Subtrahend but are closer together.

We might start with these kinds of problems:

$$23 - 19 \qquad 51 - 48 \qquad 34 - 27$$

Then we move on to these kinds of problems:

$$223 - 219 \qquad 351 - 348 \qquad 435 - 427$$

Once students use this strategy, they will be ready to plunge into more complicated problems. Although they might not use the most efficient adding strategies at first, they will gravitate to more efficient moves. In the example problem $63 - 28$, students may start with 28 and skip by tens: 38, 48, 58 plus 5 to get to 63. Another student may begin at 28 and jump 2 to get to 30, then skip by tens, 40, 50, 60 plus 3 is 63, again adding 35 in all. But over time students will realize that once they have made a jump to a "friendly" number, they can get from that number to any number in just one jump. For example, 28 plus 2 gets them to 30; then a jump of 33 gets them to 63.

Questions that are useful for the Add Instead strategy:

- How did you decide your first move?
- Did anybody use this strategy but make different jumps?
- How do you know what the answer is?

Add Instead with Fractions and Decimals

Add Instead is a great strategy for fractions and decimals because it gives students a fresh new way to think about subtraction. To choose problems, we use the same principles as we did with whole numbers, except that with fractions we are careful to choose—initially, at least—"friendly" denominators.

Decimals Example: 1.03 − .96

A student who is Adding Instead might say, "I added four hundredths to get to one whole. Then I added three more hundredths to get to 1.03. So altogether I added seven hundredths."

Recording might look like this:

Problems to get you started:

5.14 − 4.6	2 − .7	3.4 − 1.25	9.15 − 7.5

Fractions Example: 3¼ − 1¾

A student using this strategy might say, "I added ¼ to get to 2; then I added 1 to get to 3; then I added ¼ again to get to 3¼. So altogether I added 1½.

Recording might look like this:

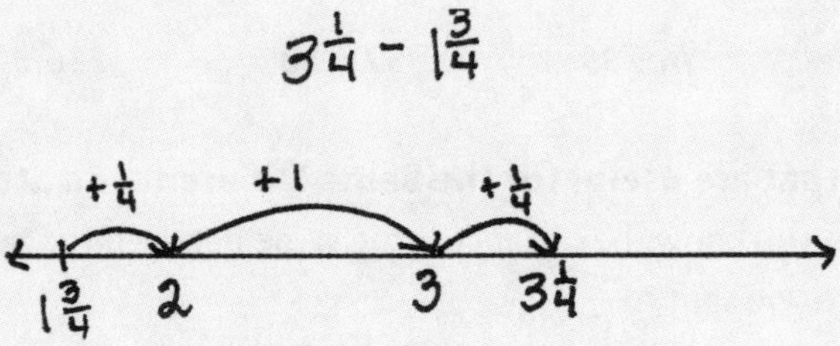

Problems to get you started (note the denominators):

4½ − 1¾ **5⅛ − 3¾** **4⅜ − 1⅞** **6⅝ − 2¾**

After students become more flexible with these denominators, you are the best judge of what to try. Every new problem will give you information about where you might go next. The sky's the limit!

4. Same Difference:

The Same Difference strategy relies on the notion of subtraction as a distance or a length that can be moved back and forth on a number line to find a convenient location for solving the problem. Because this strategy focuses on subtraction as distance, it prepares students to understand why subtraction makes sense in formulas like this when they get to algebra:

$$d = \sqrt{(x_1 - x_2)^2 + (y_1 - y_2)^2}$$

Same Difference is a truly wonderful idea for students who make sense of it, which even young children can do quite easily. Although this strategy works well for any numbers, it is one that students rarely invent for themselves, so a good way to introduce this strategy is through a class investigation. The second investigation in Chapter 9 has students investigate the Same Difference strategy and whether it will always work.

How to choose problems that invite students to use the Same Difference strategy:

Same Difference can be used with all kinds of subtraction problems, but students have to think about how much to add or subtract to make the problem easier to compute. To nudge them toward this strategy, we choose problems whose subtrahend is closer to a multiple of ten or one hundred than is the minuend.

Problems like these may tempt students to round the subtrahend and then add or subtract the same number to the minuend.

$$93 - 28 \qquad 76 - 39 \qquad 57 - 18 \qquad 236 - 188 \qquad 3456 - 687$$

Questions that are useful for the Same Difference strategy:
- How do you know the distance is the same between the numbers?
- Why did you shift to ___?
- Did anyone use this same strategy in a different way?

Same Difference with Fractions and Decimals

Same Difference is a brand new way for students to think about subtraction of decimals and fractions.

Decimals Example: 3.76 − 1.99

This is an example of a problem that the Same Difference strategy makes really easy. A student could say, "I added one one-hundredth to 1.99 and to 3.76. That changed the problem to 3.77 minus 2, so the answer is 1.77."

$$+.01 \left(\begin{array}{c} 3.76 - 1.99 \\ 3.77 - 2.00 \end{array} \right) +.01$$

$$1.77$$

or

$$3.76 - 1.99$$
$$3.77 - 2.00$$

Problems to get you started:

9.3 − 2.8	**7.6 − 3.9**	**5.75 − 1.85**	**.236 − .188**

Fractions Example: 3⅛ − 1⅞

A student might say, "I added ⅛ to both numbers. 1⅞ plus ⅛ is 2, and 3⅛ plus ⅛ is 3¼. So, 3¼ minus 2 is 1¼.

$$+\tfrac{1}{8}\left(\begin{array}{c} 3\tfrac{1}{8} - 1\tfrac{7}{8} \\ 3\tfrac{2}{8} - 2 \end{array}\right)+\tfrac{1}{8}$$

$$3\tfrac{1}{4} - 2 = 1\tfrac{1}{4}$$

Problems to get you started:

1⅖ − ⅘	**2⅜ − 1⅞**	**4⅙ − 2⅚**	**3⅓ − ⅚**

Once students get more comfortable, you can try problems like these.

5¼ − 3⅞	**53¹⁄₁₀ − 10⅘**	**4⅓ − 1⅚**	**6⅗ − 3⁹⁄₁₀**

Same Difference
with Integers*

Most students enter the upper grades with a mishmash of rules and tricks for subtracting integers but rarely have the opportunity to make sense of what is really happening. But if your students understand the Same Difference on the number line well enough to use it as a tool for their thinking, then this strategy can help them make sense of subtracting integers—maybe for the first time. The goal is to get them thinking about difference as distance.

Another challenge that students have with negative numbers is their format, and it is important for students to be flexible with this. So we have written negative numbers in three different ways: with parentheses, with the negative sign raised, and with the negative sign looking exactly like a subtraction sign.

---

* Again, the negative numbers are purposely written in the variety of ways that students may encounter them. This helps students become more flexible with symbolic notation.

Example Problem: 5 − (−3)

A student might say, "I added 3 to both numbers so that I would be subtracting 0. Negative 3 plus 3 is 0, and 5 plus 3 is 8, so 8 minus 0 is 8.

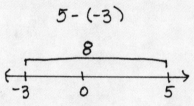

Or they might look at the number line and see that the distance between 5 and −3 is 8 units.

But is the answer positive or negative? The "Play Around with These" investigation in Chapter 9 gives students (and you) a chance to fiddle around with this and see what you can find out.

Problems to get you started:

$(−4) − 4$ $6 − {}^-5$ $−13 − (−6)$ ${}^-5 − 8$ $−7 − (−10)$

After these kinds of problems, you can challenge students with problems like these:

$−3 − \frac{2}{3}$ $5\frac{1}{2} − (−\frac{1}{4})$ $−\frac{5}{6} − (−\frac{1}{3})$ $.99 − 1$ $1.75 − (25)$

5. Break Apart by Place:

Before they have been exposed to algorithms, which teach students to start from the right in addition and subtraction, children naturally add and subtract by starting from the left (Kamii 2000). The Break Apart by Place strategy can refocus students' attention on place value and maintain the relationship among the quantities of the minuend, subtrahend, and difference. This strategy can emerge naturally from young children, who very early develop an intuition about negative numbers. It is unfortunate, though, that this happens very rarely once students have learned rules for subtraction of negative numbers (which haunt them throughout high school). As Phil Daro (2014), a principal author of the Common Core State Standards, recently observed, "Sense-making is a basic human response, and we have to be trained to suppress it." If you think it would help your students to make sense of subtraction, it is likely that you will need to introduce this strategy. Saying something like, "I saw someone solve this problem in a way I had never thought of, but I tried it on this problem. Here's what I did. . . ." Once they are introduced to the strategy, many of your students will gravitate to it—if it makes sense to them.

How to choose problems that invite Break Apart by Place:
This strategy works efficiently for nearly any whole number subtraction problem.

$$72 - 56 \qquad 81 - 27 \qquad 63 - 28 \qquad 337 - 159$$

Questions that are useful for this strategy:
- Did you think about it as 6 minus 3 or $600 - 300$?
- How do you know that 30 minus 70 is negative 40?

Break Apart by Place with Decimals

This strategy also works effectively with decimals. Most of our students have little understanding of "where the decimal point goes," and this strategy can help give them a better sense of the place value of the digits.

Decimals Example: $5.2 - 1.5$

"I took 1 away from 5, and that was 4; then I took 5 tenths away from 2 tenths and I got negative 3 tenths. So then I took 3 tenths away from 4 and I got 3 and 7 tenths."

$$5.2 - 1.5$$

$$
\begin{array}{r}
5.2 \\
-\ 1.5 \\
\hline
4 - .3 \\
3.7
\end{array}
$$

Problems to get you started:

$$5.7 - 2.9 \qquad 8.42 - .17 \qquad 13.23 - 8.54 \qquad 4.1 - 2.03$$

Students will come up with other strategies than the five main ones we have identified. Let's go back to our example problem, 63 − 28, to explore some of these strategies.

Round both numbers: Some students will round both numbers to make the problem 60 minus 30. While 60 minus 30 is easy to solve, the problem with rounding both numbers is that it is often difficult for students to sort out what they have done and how to compensate for both changes they have made. Don't worry about this strategy if it comes up, because children will quickly gravitate to strategies that work more efficiently.

Adjust the minuend: Some students will add 5 to 63 to change the problem to 68 minus 28 for an answer of 40, then subtract the 5 that they added to the 68 for an answer of 35. It is actually a good thing for students to learn that you can change either the minuend or subtrahend to make the problem easier. They will have to look carefully at the action taken in order to know how to compensate for the changes they make.

Round the minuend: Other students will take 3 away from 63 to change the problem to 60 minus 28. Students discover pretty quickly, though, that taking away a multiple of 10 or 100 is much easier than taking away any number from a multiple of 10 or 100, so they often abandon this method early on.

You won't want to discourage any methods when they come up. Instead, celebrate students' efforts to try out different ways to make sense of subtraction. Efficiency is not the goal *at first*. A focus on efficiency too early can put students back into remembering rather than sense-making. Instead, show them how pleased and excited you are that they are solving subtraction problems in ways that make sense to them. And eventually, as students see more and more strategies, the cumbersome ones will fall by the wayside.

Inside a Seventh-Grade Classroom: Digging into a Mathematical Error

3.87 − .79

Ms. Aho has been doing Number Talks with her seventh-grade students for several months. Today, she writes 3.87 − .79 on the document camera, then waits as students work to solve the problem mentally.

As they solve the problem, students quietly put their fist on their chest with a thumb up to indicate that they have a way of solving the problem. Some students

who have found one solution look for additional ways to solve the problem and indi-
cate each new way by showing an additional finger. Ms. Aho waits until everyone has
had time to solve the problem, knowing that those who finish quickly will dig into the
problem in search of additional solutions.

When most thumbs are up, she asks, "Is anyone willing to share the answer they
got?" (Previously she had talked with students about the importance of not indicating
if they agree with an answer that is offered so that everyone has an opportunity to
share their answer and she has the added benefit of informally assessing if students
are successful at solving the problem.) Students offer two answers, 3.08 and 3.06,
which she records without comment.

Ms. Aho: Who is willing to convince us that you have an answer
that makes sense by telling us what you did? (She calls
on Michelle.) Which answer are you defending?

Michelle: I'm defending 3 and 8 hundredths. I took 80 hundredths
from 3 and 87 hundredths and got 3 and 7 hundredths.
But I took away too much, so I added back the extra 1
hundredth that I had taken away, and my answer is 3
and 8 hundredths.

$$3.87 - .79$$

$$\text{Michelle} \quad \begin{array}{r} 3.87 \\ -.80 \\ \hline 3.07 \\ +.01 \\ \hline 3.08 \end{array}$$

(Note: When Ms. Aho first started working with decimals, students always read dec-
imals like 3.87 as "Three point eight seven" [which is an almost universal response
from middle and high school students]. But she knows that reading decimals like
that can obscure the value of the digits, so the first time the issue arose, she said, "But
what does that really mean?" or "Can you read the number without saying the word
point?" So, at this time in the year, this habit had been happily eradicated.)

There are several questions that Ms. Aho could ask at this moment. They include
"How many of you solved it the same way as Michelle did?" This question gives her a

quick assessment of who is using which strategy. Also, if there are only a few hands up, then she knows that there are other strategies that students have used. Or she could ask, "Who has a question for Michelle?" In this case, Ms. Aho asked both questions.

A few students raised their hands to show that they had used the same method as Michelle, so Ms. Aho knew that students had used other strategies. Before moving on to another strategy, though, she asked, "Who has a question for Michelle?" Jamie raised his hand.

Jamie:	I sort of did it the same way, but I didn't get the same answer, and I know what I did wrong now.

Again, Ms. Aho could go a couple of different directions. Jamie did not have a question about Michelle's strategy; rather, he had learned something from Michelle's strategy that he wanted to share. Ms. Aho could have said, "Jamie, hold that thought, and we will come back to you. Does anyone have a question for Michelle?" But instead, Ms. Aho chose to follow Jamie.

Ms. Aho to Jamie:	Do you want to share that with us? (Jamie nods.)
Jamie:	I started just like Michelle, and I took 80 hundredths from 3 and 87 hundredths, and I got 3 and 7 hundredths. Then I took away the 1 hundredth that I added to the 79 hundredths and got 3 and 6 hundredths. But now I know that I should have added back the one hundredth because Michelle helped me see that I really took away too much to start with.

Ms. Aho has worked hard to create a culture where mistakes are seen as opportunities for new learning rather than something to be ashamed of, and her students are frequently willing to talk about the mistakes they have made. She also knows that talking about Jamie's mistake can help to illuminate ideas that might be confusing for other students as well.

> **Ms. Aho:** Jamie, can you help us understand why you added the .01 instead of subtracting it, or would you like for someone else to try to explain?
>
> **Jamie:** At first I thought I had to subtract the .01 because I added it to .79. But now I see that when I added it to .79 I subtracted too much. I was supposed to take away .79 and I took away .80. So I had to add the extra .01 that I took away to my answer.

Now Ms. Aho uses an instructional strategy that is valuable in Number Talks when there is a complicated issue.

> **Ms. Aho to the class:** Would you take a minute to talk to people around you about what Jamie just explained?

Kids huddle and talk quietly. When the talk dies down, which is only a couple of minutes later, Ms. Aho calls the class back together.

> **Ms. Aho:** Does anyone have a question for Jamie?

No one does, but she knows better than to think that everyone has followed Jamie's thinking. So she perseveres:

> **Ms. Aho:** Jamie, is it okay if we see if someone else can try to explain what your mistake was?
>
> **Jamie:** Okay.
>
> **Ms. Aho:** Does anyone think they can help us understand what Jamie's mistake was?

Jennifer volunteers.

Jennifer: I think Jamie added .01 to .79 and got .8. Then he took .8 away from 3.87 and got 3.07. Then he subtracted .01, but she should have added.

Ms. Aho: Why should he have added instead of subtracting?

Jennifer: Because .8 is larger than .79 and he took .8 away, so she needed to add it back in.

Ms. Aho: Oh, now this is getting interesting! Are you saying Jamie should have added the one hundredth *twice*? (Turns to the class.) So Jamie and Jennifer both think that after Jamie added the .01 to the .79, he should have added .01 again to the answer after he subtracted? Turn and talk to some people around you. See if you can figure out why it makes sense to add the .01 twice: first to the .79 and then to the 3.07 after she subtracted.

The students talk in small groups for another few minutes. Ms. Aho knew this was an important use of the Number Talk time because adding twice is counterintuitive to many students. She had seen this kind of error before and believed that untangling the issue would help students develop a greater understanding of how subtraction works.

Ms. Aho: Who did this problem a different way?

After this Number Talk, Ms. Aho will think about what problem to do next. Her students seemed comfortable using multiple strategies for subtracting with decimals, yet their thumbs did not come up as quickly as she had hoped. She decided that posing a similar problem would give additional practice that she knew they needed and would provide an opportunity for Jamie (and others) to confront his earlier mistake. She decided to pose the problem 4.73 − .89 next.

While you may start with the same Number Talk at fifth or tenth grade, the trajectory will probably be different because you will base each subsequent Number Talk on what you have learned about students' thinking. A big part of the power of Number Talks is that students can discover things that we, as teachers, might never have thought of. In this way, Number Talks are generative for students and teachers alike in developing new understandings about how numbers and operations work. And while the traditional subtraction algorithm obscures place value, Number Talks depend on students using and understanding place value relationships. Therefore, while subtraction Number Talks help students learn to reason flexibly as they subtract, they also serve to develop students' understanding of important mathematical ideas that go beyond subtraction.

5 | Multiplication Across the Grades

In this chapter we focus on generalizable strategies for multiplication that are useful in helping students understand the properties of arithmetic and that provide a foundation for algebra. But first, we need to think about how Number Talks help students learn multiplication problems with single-digit factors.

Number Talks and Multiplication Facts

Mastery of addition and multiplication "facts" has been a dilemma for as long we can remember. While there is widespread agreement that quick access to these facts—which we prefer to think of as number *combinations*—is vital for success in math, the customary approach has been to encourage rote memorization. Flash cards and timed tests have continued to make regular appearances in US classrooms as early as the second grade despite decades of evidence that, at best, they don't work very well—as any middle and high school teacher knows. Timed tests, in particular, which cause many children to dislike and avoid math, have long been associated with math anxiety (Tobias 1978). And as Jo Boaler (2014) points out, "Occurring in students from an early age, math anxiety and its effects are exacerbated over time, leading to low achievement, math avoidance, and negative experiences of math throughout life" (469). Early in our careers, we, too, were expected to use these methods, but, knowing what we know now, we so wish we could have those students back again!

The following analogy helped us make sense of why timed tests and flash cards don't support children's proficiency with numbers and got us thinking about how to help students master number facts in a different way:

Imagine a stack of cards like this:

$$b \odot g$$

Eight different letters are randomly paired with each of the other letters to produce 64 different cards; each combination has an "answer" written on the back of the card (for $b \odot g$, by the way, the answer is z).

Suppose we are asked to memorize the answers to all 64 combinations. We know the names of the letters, and with a little practice we can remember that $b \odot g = z$. We might even notice that $g \odot b$ also is equal to z. We practice, over and over. But it's hard to remember them all. And imagine if someone timed us to see how fast we could say them!

This scenario is not unlike what learning basic facts is like for many children. One could argue that this analogy isn't fair—that letters and numbers are different because combinations of letters are unrelated to their answer, while numbers have relationships that can help the answers make sense. We agree completely! Without inherent relationships, letter combinations can *only* be learned by rote memorization or mnemonic devices—hard to learn and easy to forget.

We have come to realize, however, that flash cards and timed tests treat the number combinations *as if* they are, like letter combinations, unrelated to their answers. But number combinations do have inherent patterns and relationships that, when explored and understood, help students learn and use the multiplication facts with flexibility and confidence.

We are sometimes asked, "Does it matter if students learn multiplication facts through Number Talks or with flash cards and timed tests, just as long as they learn them?" Yes, it matters! We might think flash cards and timed tests can't hurt, but they can. They give students a false idea about what mathematics is and about what it means to be good at math. (For further information about the damage done by timed tests, see Boaler 2014.)

Number Talks can give every student the chance to master—and understand—the multiplication facts. Here is a brief glimpse into a seventh-grade class as students are engaged in a Number Talk:

7×8

As soon as 7×8 is written on the document camera, a bunch of thumbs go up. After waiting for everyone's thumb, the teacher calls on a student who says, "56."

Mr. Hoffman:	Did anyone get a different answer? (No one admits to it.)
Mr. Hoffman:	Who can explain how you got it?
Susanne:	I just knew it.
Mr. Hoffman:	Did anyone think about 7 times 8 in a different way? (Again, no one. But there are probably a few students in the room who counted by 7 eight times, keeping track on their fingers under the desk, and others who just waited for someone else to respond.)
Mr. Hoffman:	It sounds like everyone just knows that 7 times 8 equals 56. But let's explore this a little bit and think about how you could work it out if you didn't know. So, pretend you don't know. What would be an easy way to figure out 7 times 8 quickly? (The teacher waits for what seems too long until enough hands are up.)
Marta:	I know 7 times 7 is 49, so I added one more 7 and got 56.
Mr. Hoffman:	Why did you add one more 7?
Marta:	I needed eight 7s, but I only had seven.
Mr. Hoffman:	So you added one more 7 to 49. How did you do that?
Marta:	I know 7 times 7 is 49, so I added 1 to 49 to get 50, then I added 6 more.
Mr. Hoffman:	Who thought about it a different way? (No one.) Well, let's think about this. How else *could* we do it if we didn't know what 7 times 8 is?
Jacob:	Well, 4 times 7 is 28, so if you add 28 and 28, that would be the same.
Teresa:	10 times 7 is 70, and you could take away two 7s, or 14, and that's 56.

When you engage your students in a Number Talk like this, continue asking, "How else?" and "How else?" And don't forget to ask students why their strategies make sense when you think it will help others understand.

But what are the students learning during this Number Talk that they don't learn through flash cards and timed tests? They are learning that they have mathematical ideas worth listening to—and so do their classmates. They are learning not to give up when they can't get an answer right away because they are realizing that speed isn't important. They are learning about relationships between quantities and what multiplication really means. They are using the properties of the real numbers that will support their understanding of algebra.

And what about the Mathematical Practices? Here are just a few that students used during this one brief Number Talk:

- Make sense of quantities and their relationships [MP2]
- Justify their conclusions [MP3]
- Communicate precisely to others [MP6]

Multiplication Across the Grades

Multiplication Number Talks are brimming with potential to help students learn the properties of real numbers (although they don't know it yet), and over time, the properties come to life in students' own strategies.

Before this can happen, though, we have a delicate problem, especially for many middle and high school students. If, after 8 or more years in school, a student has little experience reasoning about arithmetic and only the traditional algorithms to rely on, then we need to give patient attention to helping them break free.

Liberating Students from Their Dependence on Rote Procedures

When students have had little experience thinking with numbers, it is natural that they resort to traditional algorithms. We have devoted a small section of this chapter to exploring how to help students move into sense-making if they get stuck in the algorithm. We have also devoted a section to this in Chapter 10.

There is no direct route here; every class is different. Students come with varying understandings, experiences, and confidence in themselves as mathematical thinkers. And they don't often come to us with a disposition to work on multiplication in ways other than the standard algorithm. It can help to just talk with your students honestly about this. For a glimpse at what this might look like, we offer the following excerpt from a Number Talk that Ruth did when she was visiting an eighth-grade class in California. We enter about ten minutes into a Number Talk where these eighth graders are doing mental computation to solve the problem 12 × 18. Number Talks were brand new to this group of students.

12 × 18

Students have given four answers that are listed on the board: 116, 206, 216, and 204.

Ruth:	Who is willing to explain how you got one of these answers and why it makes sense?
Keanon:	I did 10 times 18 . . . Well . . . I broke the 12 into 10 plus 2, and then I did 10 times 18 and got 180. Then I did 2 times 18.
Ruth:	Which answer are you defending?
Keanon:	216.
Ruth:	Okay, so when you multiplied 2 by 18, what did you get?
Keanon:	36. So I added 180 and 36.

$$12 \times 18$$
$$(10+2) \times 18$$
$$10 \times 18 = 180$$
$$2 \times 18 = +36$$
$$\overline{216}$$

Ruth:	How did you add them?
Keanon:	I added 0 and 6. Then I added 8 and 3, then I put the 1 by the other 1, and I got 216.

Ruth notices that Keanon slipped right back into the traditional algorithm when adding the partial products. She knows that this happens frequently when students are becoming familiar with Number Talks. Initially, they have a tendency to think creatively about the topic at hand—in this case, multiplication—but fall back on the familiar traditional algorithms without seeming to notice. She decides not to mention this now because Keanon had at first been reluctant to share his thinking.

Ruth:	How many of you used the same method as Keanon? (One other hand goes up.)
	That means there are more strategies out there. Who is willing to share a different one? Elizabeth, what answer are you defending?
Elizabeth:	Well, I moved the 12 under the 18. And I did 2 times 8 and got 16, so I put down the 2 and put the 1 above the 1.

Ruth writes 12 × 18, with the 12 under the 18, and records what Elizabeth has said so far.

Ruth, turning to the class:	Elizabeth has used what we call the "traditional algorithm." How many of the rest of you used the traditional algorithm? (Most of the students raise their hands.)
	Most of you—that's the way I was taught to multiply, too. And I was already teaching before I learned that there are easier ways to multiply. So, I have some bad news for you: we were all taught to work way too hard. Number Talks help us learn to work smart and efficiently, and I know you'll all learn to do that. As soon as the problems get bigger, the traditional algorithm is going to become almost impossible to do mentally. Did anybody do it a different way?
Sean:	Well, I did it differently, but I don't know if it's right.
Ruth:	Thanks for being willing to share when you aren't sure! Which answer are you defending, Sean?
Sean:	216.
Ruth:	Can you explain what you did and why it makes sense?
Sean:	I knew 12 times 12 is 144. And I had six 12s left, and I knew 6 times 12 is 72. So I added 144 and 72.
Ruth:	How did you add 144 and 72?
Sean:	I did it like Keanon. I moved the 72 under the 144. 4 and 2 is 6, and 7 plus 4 is 11. So I carried the 1 and I got 216.

> **Ruth:** Oh—you used the traditional algorithm for addition. Does anybody have a question for Sean? (No one does.)
>
> **Ruth:** Who would like to tell how they got a different answer and why it makes sense? (No one does.)

This doesn't surprise Ruth because she has seen many students change their mind after becoming convinced by others' explanations. She knows that as students become comfortable with Number Talks, they begin to share mistakes that they made.

> **Ruth:** Thank you for sharing your thinking today. Maybe tomorrow more of you will have a chance to share.

Ruth now is thinking about what problem to do tomorrow. She decides that 12 × 15 might be a good way to go, because it is enough like 12 × 18 that students can build on the methods that were shared today.

In the rest of this chapter, we use the problem 12 × 16 to demonstrate four multiplication strategies, most of which work efficiently across the rational numbers. Several of these strategies are ones that students usually come up with on their own.

Four Strategies for Multiplication

Factor × Factor = Product

12 × 16

1. Break a Factor into Two or More Addends:

"I broke the 16 into 10 and 6. First I multiplied 10 times 12 and got 120. Next I multiplied 6 times 12 and got 72. Then I added 120 to 72 and got 192."

$$12 \times 16$$

$$12 \times 16 = 12 \times (10 + 6)$$
$$= (10 + 6) \times 12$$

$$10 \times 12 = 120$$
$$6 \times 12 = \underline{72}$$
$$192$$

2. Factor a Factor:

"I know 16 equals 4 times 2 times 2. First I did 4 times 12, and that was 48. Then I did 48 times 2, and I got 96. And then I did 96 times 2, and I got 192."

$$12 \times 16$$

$$12 \times 16 = 12 \times (4 \times 2 \times 2)$$
$$12 \times 4 = 48$$
$$\times 2$$
$$96 \times 2 = 192$$

or

If students are ready for an explicit connection to more symbolic recording, we might also record like this to emphasize the associative property of multiplication:

$$12 \times 16$$

$$12 \times 16 = 12 \times (4 \times 2 \times 2)$$
$$= (12 \times 4) \times (2 \times 2)$$
$$= 48 \times (2 \times 2)$$
$$= (48 \times 2) \times 2$$
$$= 96 \times 2$$
$$= 192$$

3. Round a Factor and Adjust:

"I rounded 16 to 20, and I did 12 times 20 and got 240. Then I took away four 12s, or 48. I took 40 from 240 and got 200; then I took away 8 more and got an answer of 192."

$$12 \times 16 \quad (16 = 20 - 4)$$

$$12 \times 20 = 240$$
$$12 \times 4 = 48 \begin{cases} 40 \\ +8 \end{cases}$$

$$240 - 40 = 200$$
$$200 - 8 = 192$$

or

$$12 \times 16$$

$$12 \times (20-4)$$

$$(12 \times 20) - (12 \times 4)$$

$$240 - 48$$

$$192$$

4. Halving and Doubling:

"I doubled 12 and cut 16 in half, so I changed the problem to 24 times 8. Then I kept halving and doubling; so I got 48 times 4 and then 96 times 2, and my answer is 192."

$$12 \times 16$$

$$12 \times 16 = 24 \times 8$$
$$= 48 \times 4$$
$$= 96 \times 2$$
$$= 192$$

Developing the Multiplication Strategies in Depth

1. Break a Factor into Addends:

This is the strategy that Keanon used above. Breaking a factor into addends and using the distributive property allows us to turn problems that seem too hard to think about into much easier problems to solve. For example, mentally thinking about the problem 23×13 is challenging. But when we break 23 into $20 + 3$, multiplying is much easier.

To encourage the use of this strategy, we purposefully select numbers that can be divided into addends that are easy to think about, such as two plus something, or ten plus something, or twenty-five plus something, or fifty plus something.

Students are often encouraged to decompose numbers into tens and ones, but this is not the only way to make a problem easier by breaking a factor into addends. One high school student, for example, when doing 18×5, chose to break 5 into $2 + 2 + 1$. This made the problem $18 \times (2 + 2 + 1)$, which was easier for her to think about.

This strategy can be especially useful when students cling to the traditional algorithm and need to be coaxed to make the problem easier to think about, and it brings the distributive property of multiplication over addition to life for students.

How to choose problems that invite students to Break a Factor into Addends:

We try to select two numbers where changing just one factor makes the problem pretty easy to solve mentally. We might start with problems that can be changed to ten plus something. Problems such as:

12×6 $\qquad$ 13×8 $\qquad$ 14×12 $\qquad$ 12×13 $\qquad$ 13×7

Many students will then be able to apply this strategy to two-digit-by-two-digit multiplication, such as:

12×14 $\qquad$ 14×25 $\qquad$ 26×48 $\qquad$ 52×18 $\qquad$ 13×26

To further challenge your students you can gradually move a factor farther away from a "friendly" number—for example, 27 times a number, or 53 times a number.

Questions that are useful for the strategy of Break a Factor into Addends:

- How did changing 27 into 25 plus 2 help you solve the problem?
- Why didn't breaking up the 27 change the value of the answer?
- How did you decide to break the factor up that way?

A Note About Recording

When you are recording the Break a Factor into Addends strategy, the geometric representation of the multiplication of two numbers as dimensions of a rectangle creates a wonderful image that helps students better understand their own strategies. It also can become a powerful problem-solving tool. The visual image is so useful in helping students understand the distributive property of multiplication over addition that we have included in Chapter 9 an investigation about geometric representations in multiplication.

Breaking a Factor into Addends with Fractions and Decimals

This strategy is particularly efficient with decimals and fractions if one of the factors is a whole number and the other is a fraction or mixed number with a denominator that is "friendly" with the other factor. For example, ⅓ is "friendly" with 12 because 12 can be broken into three equal parts. To invite this strategy, you can get them started with problems like these:

5.5 × 12	**12.25 × 12**	**5.1 × 30**	**6.25 × 24**
2⅓ × 12	**1¾ × 16**		

and challenge them with problems like these:

3⅞ × 16	**11.75 × 40**	**5.375 × 24**	**14⅘ × 100**

2. Factor a Factor:

To encourage the use of this strategy, we purposefully select numbers that have several factors. Factoring a number like 16 into 4 × 4 or 2 × 8 often makes it easier to rearrange the factors so that problems are easier to solve. Not only does this strategy help students learn to factor with ease, but it also lays the foundation for them to understand the associative property of multiplication $(a \times b) \times c = a \times (b \times c)$.

How to choose problems that invite students to use the Factor a Factor strategy:
We might start with numbers that have 2, 3, or 5 as factors.

12 × 6, where students might do **2 × 6 × 6, for 2 × 36**, or **72**

6 × 8, where students might do **6 × 4 × 2, for 24 × 2**, or **48**

15 × 8, where they might do **3 × 5 × 8, for 3 × 40**, or **120**

12 × 13, where they might do **3 × 4 × 13, for 3 × 52**, or **156**

Once they have the idea, many students will naturally apply this strategy to larger numbers, such as:

- 81 × 25, which some will change to 9 × 9 × 25, then multiply 9 × 25 to get 225, and then multiply 10 × 225 for 2250. Finally, they will subtract 225 to get 2025.

$$81 \times 25$$
$$(9 \times 9) \times 25$$
$$9 \times (9 \times 25)$$
$$9 \times 225$$
$$10 \times 225 = 2250$$
$$2250 - 225 = 2025$$

- 250 × 28, which some will change into 25 × 10 × 28, then multiply 10 × 28 for 280, then multiply 280 × 25 by thinking of it as ¼ of 28,000, or 7000.

$$250 \times 28$$
$$25 \times 10 \times 28$$
$$10 \times 28 = 280$$
$$280 \times 25 \quad \overset{\circ\,\circ\,\circ}{\left(100 \div 4 = 25 \right)}$$
$$280 \times 100 = 28,000$$
$$28,000 \div 4 = 7,000$$

Here are a few other problems you might begin with:

14 × 25   25 × 16   51 × 14   18 × 26

Questions that are useful for the Factor a Factor strategy:

- How did you decide which number to factor?
- How did you decide which factors to use?
- How did factoring ___ make the problem easier?
- Why does this work?

3. Round a Factor and Adjust:

When multiplying mentally, rounding one of the factors to get to a multiple of 10 and then compensating makes many problems easier to solve. For example, given the problem 29 × 7, many students will round 29 to 30. Since 3 times 7 is 21, 30 times 7 is 210. They then have thirty 7s, so they take 7 from 210 for an answer of 203.

$$
\begin{array}{r}
29 \times 7 \\
30 \times 7 = 210 \\
- 7 \\
\hline
203
\end{array}
$$

In addition to making it easy to turn "messy" numbers into "friendly" numbers, this strategy also brings the distributive and commutative properties to life as students come to understand their usefulness. This builds the foundation for using these properties with symbols in algebra and beyond.

How to choose problems that invite students to Round a Factor and Adjust:
To encourage the use of this Round and Adjust strategy, we chose problems where just one of the factors is close to ten, such as these:

12×9 $\qquad$ 6×19 $\qquad$ 21×7 $\qquad$ 8×13 $\qquad$ 9×23

Once students know that they can round a factor and then adjust, they naturally apply this strategy with larger numbers like the following:

28×13 $\qquad$ 27×18 $\qquad$ 48×26 $\qquad$ 39×23 $\qquad$ 197×56

Teaching Tip

Even though we have purposefully selected problems where just one factor is close to a power of ten, students sometimes round both factors. Once they have done this, though, it is sometimes difficult for them to figure out how to compensate for both moves. Don't worry about this, because students will quickly realize that rounding only one factor works more efficiently. If they do round both factors, however, it is interesting and fun—if not efficient—to figure out how to compensate. The geometric representation investigation in Chapter 9 will give students an interesting way to think about this.

Questions that are useful for the Round a Factor and Adjust strategy:

- How did rounding the factor to _____ make this problem easier?
- How did you know what to subtract (or add)?
- How did you decide which factor to round?

Round a Factor and Adjust with Fractions and Decimals

This strategy can work with carefully chosen decimals or fractions. Thinking about 3 × 2⅞, for example, as 3 × 3 − ⅛ makes the problem much easier.

$$3 \times 2\tfrac{7}{8}$$
$$3 \times \left(3 - \tfrac{1}{8}\right)$$
$$(3 \times 3) - \left(3 \times \tfrac{1}{8}\right)$$
$$9 - \tfrac{3}{8}$$
$$8\tfrac{5}{8}$$

Similarly, 5 × 1.99 is more easily worked out as 5 × 2 − 5(.01).

To invite this strategy, we choose problems in which one factor is a whole number and the other is easy to round to a whole number.

5¾ × 7	4¹¹⁄₁₂ × 9	8 × 1⅚	3 × 5.8
6.97 × 8	2 × 11.95		

4. Halving and Doubling Strategy:

The Halving and Doubling strategy can be especially useful in making multiplication problems easier to solve. For example, 26 × 28 might feel daunting to solve. But if we double the 26 and halve the 28, we now have 52 × 14. If this still feels a bit daunting, we can double the 52, and halve the 14, which gives us 104 × 7. Now that's pretty easy to think about!

$$26 \times 28$$
$$52 \times 14$$
$$104 \times 7$$
$$728$$

The trouble is that we can "show" students this strategy and they can use it without understanding. But when something seems to "work" all of the time, there has to be a reason, and we want to help our students to develop dispositions to be curious and wonder about what that reason might be. When does this work? When doesn't it? Making sense of these ideas is foundational for students' algebraic reasoning—no matter what their grade—so we hope you will invest a class period to having your students learn how to seek answers to their questions by investigating. To help you enact these investigations with your students, see the section "Will It Always Work? Investigation 4: Halving and Doubling in Multiplication" in Chapter 9.

As students become more flexible with numbers, they think it is pretty easy to solve the problem 52 × 14. They may think of 50 × 14 as half of 1400, or 700, then multiply 2 × 14 for 28, and then sum 700 + 28, for a total of 728.

How to choose problems that invite students to use Halving and Doubling:
Initially we use problems with combinations of factors that can easily be halved and doubled to get close to a "friendly number." Problems like:

$$8 \times 13 \qquad 4 \times 17 \qquad 6 \times 13 \qquad 8 \times 25 \qquad 22 \times 9$$

Questions that are useful for the Halving and Doubling strategy:
- How did you decide which number to double and which number to halve?
- Why did that make it an easier problem to think about?

Halving and Doubling with Fractions and Decimals

Halving and Doubling works well with decimal problems where one number is easy to halve and halve again. For example, given the problem .36 × .8, some students halve and double to get .72 × .4, then 1.44 × .2, then 2.88 × .1, which makes an easy problem to think about. Here are some other problems where halving and doubling works nicely:

$$.8 \times 1.2 \qquad .64 \times .08 \qquad 3.26 \times .08 \qquad 7\tfrac{1}{4} \times 4 \qquad 3\tfrac{1}{8} \times 4$$
$$4.2 \times .6 \qquad .221 \times .04 \qquad 3\tfrac{1}{2} \times 8 \qquad 16 \times 6\tfrac{1}{4}$$

This is not an efficient strategy for all decimals and fractions, but you won't need to tell students this. They will figure it out on their own!

Connecting Arithmetic and Algebra

As you've seen, these four strategies bring the properties of real numbers to life (for a list of these properties, see Appendix B). If students have had many experiences using—and talking about—these properties in Number Talks, it will be easier for them to make sense of these same properties in algebra, which appear in textbooks like this:

> The Distributive Property of Multiplication over Addition:
>
> $$a(b + c) = ab + ac$$

This notation doesn't help students much. But when they understand how—and why—the properties work through Number Talks, they only need to attach the name of the property to what they already understand. The following vignette illustrates how students began to understand the distributive property during a Number Talk.

18 × 5

Miguel:	I did 10 times 5 plus 8 times five.
Ms. Ballon:	What did you get?
Miguel:	10 times 5 is 50.
Ms. Ballon:	And what did you get for 8 times 5?
Miguel:	40. So 50 and 40 is 90.

$$18 \times 5$$
$$10 \times 5 = 50$$
$$8 \times 5 = +40$$
$$\overline{ 90}$$

Ms. Ballon:	Mathematicians have a name for what you have done. They call it the distributive property of multiplication over addition. (She records this on the board.) So, Miguel, you thought about the 18 as 10 plus 8—is that right?
Miguel:	Yes.

Ms. Ballon records 10 + 8 and asks the class if Miguel changed the value of 18.

$$18 \times 5$$

$$(10 + 8) \times 5$$

> **Ms. Ballon:** Then you distributed the 5 across the 10 and 8 by first multiplying 5 times 10 and then adding 8 times 5. (She records as she says this.)

$$18 \times 5$$

$$(10 + 8) \times 5$$

$$(10 \times 5) + (8 \times 5)$$

$$50 + 40$$

I think other people used the distributive property, too, but some of you broke up 18 differently than Miguel did. For example, Marquis broke 18 into 9 plus 9 instead of 10 plus 8. We'll be using the distributive property of multiplication over addition a lot, and we'll try to notice when we do.

Also, I want to give you another way to think about this more visually, and that's with something we call area models. Because we are studying geometry, I think it might click for you.

We start with our 5 and our 18. This is called an area model because the area of the rectangle is 5 times 18, or, as we found out, 90.

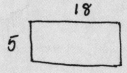

What Miguel was thinking is, he cut this 18 into 8 and 10.

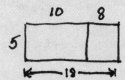

> Do you still see the 18? (Students nod.) Where is the
> 10 times 5 in the picture?
>
> **Max:** In the box with the 5 and the 10. (Ms. Ballon writes 50
> in the rectangle.)
>
> **Ms. Ballon:** What about the 8 times 5?
>
> **Students:** In the other box.

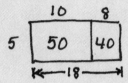

> **Ms. Ballon:** So this model can be a good tool for solving multi-
> plication problems, no matter how big the numbers
> are. If they're messy numbers, you can just take them
> apart to make numbers that are easy to think about,
> record the amounts in the different regions, and then
> add the amounts.

(Note: The optimal time to introduce students to the arithmetic properties is when they use them on their own. In fact, we feel that the best time to introduce any mathematical vocabulary is when it is used to label an idea that students understand.)

Teaching Tip: FOIL

Students are taught to multiply binomials using FOIL: "first, outside, inside, last." Most students never think about why this procedure works and then are left with no idea what to do when there are three binomials to multiply—because FOIL doesn't work. Having students connect geometric and algebraic representations helps students see the real relationships involved so that they can apply what they know about binomials to other kinds of problems. For more on this, see the section "Geometric Representations in Multiplication" in Chapter 9.

Phil Daro (2010), one of the principal authors of the Common Core State Standards, observed recently, "You can't really do mental math without doing algebra. This is algebraic reasoning at its purest level." Multiplication Number Talks provide a rich opportunity to help students understand the arithmetic properties that are essential to mathematics at all levels. Daro says:

> The nine properties are the foundation for arithmetic and the most important preparation for algebra. The exact same properties work for whole numbers, fractions, negative numbers, letters, and expressions. They are the same properties in third grade and in calculus.

Students who have experienced Number Talks come to algebra understanding the arithmetic properties because they have used them repeatedly as they reasoned with numbers in ways that made sense to them. This doesn't happen automatically, though. As students use these properties, one of our jobs as teachers is to help students connect the strategies that make sense to them to the names of properties that are the foundation of our number system.

6

Addition Across the Grades

Addition can be a good place to start your Number Talks (after dot cards, of course) if you feel like your students have little experience with mental math and need to build up their confidence. While younger students who aren't already stuck on the traditional algorithm can get enthusiastic about different ways to add, you may find that your middle or high school students feel like addition is remedial. But you may find just the opposite! As always, you and your students will work out the best place to be.

A Note About Recording: The Open Number Line

As you'll see, we often use an "open number line" as a recording strategy during Number Talks to give students a visual model for their thinking.

Open number lines have no scale and thus are not meant to be accurate measures of units. Rather, the "jumps" can be roughly proportional. A nice thing about the open number line is it allows for really large or small numbers without having to worry about individual units.

Five Strategies for Addition

Addend + Addend = Sum

Addition is intuitive to young children who, without our help, can invent many of the following strategies on their own. We have chosen $63 + 28$ to demonstrate five addition strategies that work efficiently for addition.

$$63 + 28$$

1. Round and Adjust:

"I rounded 28 to 30. Then I added 30 and 63 and got 93. Then I took away the extra 2 that I added and got 91."

$$63 + 28$$
$$63 + 30 = 93$$
$$93 - 2 = 91$$

2. Take and Give:

"I took 2 from 63 and gave it to the 28, so I made the problem $61 + 30$; then I added 61 and 30 and got 91."

$$63 + 28$$
$$63 \xrightarrow{-2} 28$$
$$61 + 30 = 91$$

3. Start from the Left:

"I added 60 and 20 and got 80; then I added 3 and 8 and got 11; then I added 80 and 11 and got 91."

$$63 + 28$$
$$60 + 20 = 80$$
$$3 + 8 = +11$$
$$\overline{91}$$

4. Break One Addend Apart:

"I added 63 and 20 and I got 83; then I added 8 and got 91."

$$63 + 28$$
$$63 + 20 = 83$$
$$+ 8$$
$$\overline{91}$$

or

"I added 60 and 28 and got 88; then I added 3 more and got 91."

$$63 + 28$$

$$60 + 28 = 88$$

$$\begin{array}{r} + 3 \\ \hline 91 \end{array}$$

Often students will combine strategies, as with this student's way of Breaking One Addend Apart and then using Take and Give to finish the problem: "I added 63 and 20 and got 83; then I took 7 from the 8 and gave it to the 83, and that made 90, so then all I had to do was add 90 plus 1, and I got 91."

$$63 + 28$$

$$63 + 20 = 83$$

$$83 + 8 = 90 + 1 = 91$$

5. Add Up:

"I started with 63 then added 20 to get to 83; then I added 7 more to get to 90; then I added the 1 that was left to get to 91."

$$63 + 28$$

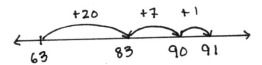

or

"I started with 28 and added 2 to get to 30; then I added 61 and got to 91."

$$63 + 28$$

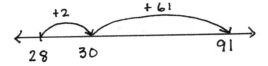

Another strategy, called Swap the Digits, is useful with very specific kinds of problems. But it is so intriguing—and its underlying properties are so important—that we have placed it in Chapter 9 instead as an investigation.

Developing the Addition Strategies in Depth

1. Round and Adjust:

Rounding one addend to a multiple of ten and then compensating/adjusting can make addition easier to think about and more efficient. Round and Adjust is popular with students because it doesn't involve "carrying." It is useful across the operations, and its use indicates growing numerical flexibility.

How to choose problems that invite students to Round and Adjust:

To nudge students toward this strategy, we look for problems in which one addend is close to a multiple of ten, one hundred, and so on. In the problem 13 + 59, for example, we hope students will think about rounding 59 to 60. We usually start with a few problems that add 8s and 9s to a two-digit number, such as:

$$13 + 9 \qquad 24 + 8 \qquad 61 + 8 \qquad 43 + 9$$

Many students then readily use this strategy for two-digit addends that are close to a multiple of ten, such as:

$$63 + 28 \qquad 71 + 39 \qquad 84 + 59 \qquad 42 + 19 \qquad 50 + 28$$

Then, with a three-digit number plus a two- or three-digit number, we look for two- or three-digit addends that are close to one hundred:

$$134 + 99 \qquad 247 + 98 \qquad 315 + 97 \qquad 468 + 99$$

Gradually, you can move the addend farther and farther away from a target multiple—for example, 54 + 28, or 81 + 17. The type of problem you choose will depend on the readiness and experience of your students.

Questions that are useful for the strategy of Round One Addend and Adjust:

- Why did you add [200] instead of [198]?

- Did you add too many or too few?
- Why did you take away _____?

Round and Adjust with Fractions and Decimals

Round and Adjust works the same with decimals and fractions as it does with whole numbers. To encourage this strategy, we use problems where one addend is close to a whole number. Here are some examples of how to vary your problems with decimals and fractions:

Decimals Example: 7.48 + 8.9

"I added .1 to 8.9 to get 9; then I added 9 to 7.48 and got 16.48. Then I took away the extra .1 that I added and got an answer of 16.38."

$$7.48 + 8.9$$
$$7.48 + 9.0 \quad = 16.48$$
$$\underline{- \ .10}$$
$$16.38$$

Problems to get you started:

6.36 + 1.8	8.9 + .57	7.48 + 3.9	23.762 + .98

Fractions Example: 2¼ + ⅞

"I added 2¼ and 1 to get 3¼. Then I took away the extra ⅛ I added and got 3⅛."

$$2\tfrac{1}{4} + \tfrac{7}{8}$$
$$2\tfrac{1}{4} + 1 = 3\tfrac{1}{4} \qquad \left(\tfrac{1}{4} = \tfrac{2}{8}\right)$$
$$3\tfrac{1}{4} - \tfrac{1}{8} = 3\tfrac{1}{8}$$

Problems to get you started:

3½ + ¾	7½ + ⅞	3⅚ + ⅓	⅓ + ⁸⁄₉

2. Take and Give:

Moving a quantity from one addend to another is another strategy (some call this "sharing") that helps students become more flexible with numbers. While we have seen students invent this strategy themselves, you can introduce it to them if they don't (see Chapter 2, "Thoughts for Successful Number Talks," #10, for suggestions).

How to choose problems that invite students to Take and Give:

To encourage this strategy, we choose problems where one addend has enough in the ones place to give something to the other addend to make it a multiple of ten or one hundred, problems like 23 + 19 (or 23 + 18 or 23 + 17).

We begin with problems where one of the addends is a single digit not far from a multiple of ten. Problems like:

$$16 + 8 \qquad 18 + 6 \qquad 29 + 7 \qquad 14 + 7$$

Once students understand how this works, they can use it with larger numbers such as these:

$$46 + 98 \qquad 89 + 45 \qquad 146 + 197 \qquad 478 + 88 \qquad 298 + 156$$

Take and Give works for any addition problem, and students easily learn to use it flexibly once they are convinced of its value.

Questions that are useful for the strategy of Take and Give:

- How did you decide how much to move?
- How did moving ___ to ___ make the problem easier?
- Did anyone use the same strategy but move a different amount?

Take and Give with Fractions and Decimals

This strategy works with decimals and fractions much like it does with whole numbers. With decimals, we choose problems with one addend close to a multiple of one or ten. With fractions, however, we select two kinds of problems: those whose addends have the same denominator and those with one addend whose denominator is a factor of the other addend's denominator.

Decimals Example Problem: 3.76 + 2.89

"I took .11 from 3.76 and put it onto 2.89, so I changed the problem to 3.65 + 3, for an answer of 6.65."

$$3.76 + 2.89$$
$$3.76 + 2.89$$
$$3.65 + 3 = 6.65$$

Problems to get you started:

23.54 + 17.97   8.9 + .56   31.67 + 18.88   3.8 + 1.44   2.96 + 5.37

Fractions Example Problem: 7⅔ + 3⁵⁄₉

I knew ³⁄₉ was ⅓, so I took ³⁄₉ from 3⁵⁄₉ and put it on 7⅔. That changed the problem to 8 + 3²⁄₉, for an answer of 11²⁄₉.

$$7\tfrac{2}{3} + 3\tfrac{5}{9} \quad \left(\tfrac{3}{9} = \tfrac{1}{3} \right)$$
$$7\tfrac{2}{3} + 3\tfrac{5}{9}$$
$$8 + 3\tfrac{2}{9}$$
$$11\tfrac{2}{9}$$

Problems to get you started:

2¾ + 6¾   5³⁄₅ + 1⁷⁄₁₀   6²⁄₅ + 3⁴⁄₅   4⅔ + ³⁄₆   7⅝ + ⁷⁄₁₆

3. Start from the Left

Research has shown that young children naturally approach addition by working from left to right—adding, for example, the hundreds first, then the tens—but abandon this natural inclination when they encounter the traditional US algorithm in which they are taught to work from right to left (Kamii 2000). Adding from left to right helps students maintain both the value of the digits and the overall quantities involved. Consider, for example, how a student might think about 34 + 55:

"I added 30 and 50 and got 80; then I added 4 and 5 and got 9; 80 plus 9 is 89."

When students think about 3 as 30, the place value of the digits is not lost. Similarly, when adding 3.6 + 2.3, students who add from the left say, "3 plus 2 is 5; 6 tenths and 3 tenths is 9 tenths. So my answer is 5 and 9 tenths." Once again, in the traditional algorithm, however, place value gets lost in the practice of adding columns of place value–neutral digits.

How to choose problems that invite students to Start from the Left:
To encourage students to Start from the Left, we select problems in which the addends are *not* close to a multiple or power of ten. These problems are typical examples:

    43 + 56   54 + 35   24 + 67   37 + 36   62 + 47

Once students understand how to Start from the Left, they readily apply it to larger problems such as:

    376 + 523   274 + 153   277 + 432   117 + 356   1834 + 2363

Questions that are useful for the Start from the Left strategy:
- How did you decide where to start?
- How did place value help you solve this problem?
- How did you keep track when [70 and 50] was more than 100?

Start from the Left with Fractions and Decimals

Start from the Left works for decimals and fractions much as it does with whole numbers. It is probably a good idea, however, for students to first have experience with this strategy using whole numbers because of students' general lack of understanding of the meaning of fractional parts.

For decimals, we select problems with addends *not* close to multiples of one or ten. We also mix problems that require regrouping with those that do not. For fractions, we begin by choosing addends with common denominators or addends in which one denominator is a factor of the other.

Decimals Example Problem: 3.63 + 2.16

"3 plus 2 is 5. Then I added .6 [we hope they say "six-tenths" instead of "point six"] to .1 and got .7; then .03 plus .06 is .09. So my answer is 5.79."

$$3.63 + 2.16$$
$$3 + 2 = 5$$
$$.6 + .1 = .7$$
$$.03 + .06 = .09$$
$$5 + .7 + .09 = 5.79$$

Problems to get you started:

4.38 + 6.31 **3.46 + 4.33** **7.26 + 3.93** **1.036 + 2.35**

Fractions Example Problem: $3\frac{5}{8} + 7\frac{3}{8}$

"3 plus 7 is 10; and $\frac{5}{8}$ plus $\frac{3}{8}$ is $\frac{8}{8}$, and that's 1 whole, so the answer is 11."

$$3\frac{5}{8} + 7\frac{3}{8}$$
$$3 + 7 = 10$$
$$\frac{5}{8} + \frac{3}{8} = \frac{8}{8} = 1$$
$$10 + 1 = 11$$

Problems to get you started:

$3\frac{5}{9} + 5\frac{2}{9}$ **$4\frac{3}{5} + 2\frac{3}{5}$** **$1\frac{7}{8} + 6\frac{3}{4}$** **$3\frac{1}{3} + 8\frac{5}{6}$**

4. Break One Addend Apart:

Adding any number to a multiple of ten with ease helps students reason more flexibly with numbers. Often preceded by learning to add multiples of ten (e.g., 30 + 40), breaking just one of the addends apart is an important step forward. Nearly any problem works with this strategy. It is important to remember that there is no "best" way to do this; students will break numbers apart in ways that make sense to them.

How to choose problems that invite students to Break One Addend Apart:

Nearly any addition problem lends itself to Breaking One Addend Apart.

Here are some problems to get you started:

15 + 23 **25 + 36** **37 + 49** **54 + 73** **53 + 38** **64 + 37**

When students are comfortable breaking apart one of the addends, they will do it with larger problems as well. Some good problems to start with are:

$237 + 314$ $456 + 238$ $328 + 234$ $183 + 276$ $1457 + 523$

About Recording to Highlight the Properties of Real Numbers

Earlier in the book we talked about how Number Talks use the same properties that underlie algebra. Unless we make those properties explicit to students, they won't realize what they are doing, but the properties are much more understandable to students when connected to thinking they have already done.

Consider the problem $56 + 47$, when a student has said this about his method: "I added 47 and 50 and I got 97; then I added the 6 left over from the 50 to 97 and got 103."

You have several different options for recording, including the open number line. But an additional option is to choose to use the recording to highlight the properties of arithmetic.

We have found it best to first record exactly what the student has said. So, we might record first like this:

$$56 + 47$$
$$50 + 47 = 97$$
$$+ 6$$
$$\overline{103}$$

After the student has agreed that your recording represents her thinking, you can say something like: "You used two important properties when you solved it this way. Let's take a look."

$$56 + 47$$
$$(50 + 6) + 47$$
$$(6 + 50) + 47 \quad \text{commutative property of addition}$$
$$6 + (50 + 47) \quad \text{associative property of addition}$$
$$6 + 97$$
$$97 + 6 \quad \text{commutative property of addition}$$
$$103$$

Questions that are useful for the strategy of Break One Addend Apart:

- How did you decide which number to break apart?
- How did adding ____ instead of ____ make the problem easier?
- How did you keep track mentally of what you did?
- Did anyone use the same strategy but break a number up differently?

Break One Addend Apart with Fractions and Decimals

This strategy can work as effectively with decimals as with whole numbers.

Decimals Example Problem: 4.57 + 5.83

"I added 4 to 5.83 and got 9.83; then I added .5 and got 10.33. Then I added .07 and got 10.4."

$$4.57 + 5.83$$
$$5.83 + 4 = 9.83$$
$$+ .5$$
$$\overline{10.33}$$
$$+ .07$$
$$\overline{10.40}$$

Problems to get you started:

.23 + .57	.354 + .33	1.07 + .68	23.51 + .36
16.204 + .26	13.38 + .73		

Break One Addend Apart helps students think about a mixed number as the sum of a whole number and a fraction; it works best with two mixed numbers.

Fractions Example Problem: 3⅙ + 9⅔

"I added 9 to 3⅙, and I got 12⅙. Then, I knew that ⅔ equals 4/6, so I added 12⅙ and 4/6 to get 12⅚. So my answer is 12⅚.

$$3\tfrac{1}{6} + 9\tfrac{2}{3} \quad \left(\tfrac{2}{3} = \tfrac{4}{6}\right)$$
$$3\tfrac{1}{6} + 9 = 12\tfrac{1}{6}$$
$$+ \tfrac{4}{6}$$
$$\overline{12\tfrac{5}{6}}$$

To encourage this strategy, we usually use two mixed numbers whose proper fractions sum to less than 1 and whose denominators are relatively friendly.

$5\frac{5}{12} + 3\frac{1}{4}$ $2\frac{3}{8} + 2\frac{1}{4}$ $3\frac{5}{12} + 1\frac{1}{6}$ $7\frac{3}{10} + 4\frac{2}{5}$

5. Add Up:

Add Up is very closely related to Break One Addend Apart, but with Add Up, students often break one addend into several parts. Although this strategy works with or without a number line, as you'll see, using a number line can help students visualize addition with both large and small numbers.

How to choose problems that invite students to Add Up:

Add Up works efficiently for nearly any problem. Here are some problems that will get you started:

$18 + 7$ $19 + 6$ $39 + 23$ $68 + 27$ $43 + 39$ $16 + 59$

Once they are comfortable using the strategy of Add Up with two-digit numbers, students will use the strategy with larger problems such as:

$258 + 36$ $547 + 34$ $546 + 28$ $351 + 439$ $1348 + 143$

Questions that are useful for the strategy of Add Up:
- How did you decide which number to start with?
- Why did you jump ___?
- How did you keep track of the moves or jumps you made?

Add Up with Fractions and Decimals

Add Up is a strategy that also works well with both decimals and fractions. For decimal problems we choose, as with whole numbers, problems in which one addend is close to a multiple or power of ten (in this case, 10^0 or 10^1).

Decimals Example Problem: $1.09 + .83$

"I started with 1.09 and added .01 to get to 1.1, then I added .8 to get to 1.9 and then added .02 to get to 1.92."

$$1.09 + .83$$

$$1.09 + .01 = 1.1$$
$$+ .8$$
$$\overline{1.9 + .02 = 1.92}$$

or

We have found the more visual empty number line to be particularly useful in recording when students use the Add Up strategy for decimals:

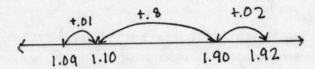

Another student might say, "I started with .83 and added .07 to get to .9; then I added 1.02 to get to 1.92."

Recording would look like this:

$$1.09 + .83$$

.83   .90   1.92
+.07   +1.02

Problems to get you started:

.97 + .34   .38 + .57   .63 + .29   1.059 + .223
2.39 + .43   7.06 + .48

With fractions, we choose addends with common denominators, or where one denominator is a factor of the other denominator.

Fractions Example Problem: 2¾ + ¾

"I started with 2¾ and added ¼ to get to 3; then I had ¾ left, but I knew that was

½, so I added ½ to 3 to get to 3½."

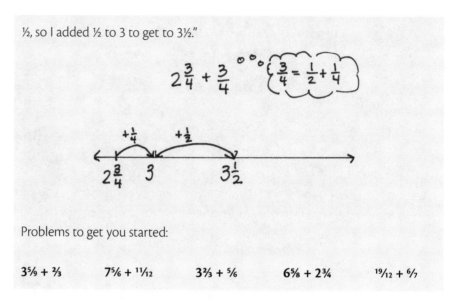

Problems to get you started:

3⅝ + ⅔   7⅚ + ¹¹⁄₁₂   3⅔ + ⅚   6⅝ + 2¾   ¹⁹⁄₁₂ + ⁶⁄₇

Once you have focused on subtraction and addition with Number Talks, your students are likely to have embraced the idea that there are many different ways to solve arithmetic problems. And they will know that they can make sense of problems in their own ways. They are also likely to bring a spirit of anticipation and inquiry as you move into the other operations with Number Talks.

CHAPTER 7

Division Across the Grades

More than 30 years ago, Richard Anderson, then president of the Mathematical Association of America, spoke at a meeting of the American Association for the Advancement of Science, where he predicted that "when computers and calculators truly come of age in the schools, paper and pencil long division will probably be 'as dead as a dodo bird'" (Maier 1982). More than a decade later, Gene Maier (1982) of the Math Learning Center wrote "Long Division: Dead as a Dodo Bird," where he, like Anderson, emphasized that there is no longer a job in the world—not one single job—where someone does long division with paper and pencil; not one job, that is, other than teaching. But here we are, more than three decades later, still spending up to two years of instructional time on a procedure that is hard to learn and easy to do incorrectly. And sadly, the meaning of division, which is what students need to learn, is lost in the shuffle.

There are some small signs that progress is being made toward Maier's vision. There is no specific reference, for example, to division of polynomials in the Common Core State Standards. Perhaps, in the not too distant future, students will be unburdened from having to spend inordinate amounts of time memorizing long and complicated mathematical procedures that they don't understand and that are always done by machines in the world of today. It's exciting to think about how much time this would afford students to play with and explore mathematical ideas as they engage in the truly inviting and exciting endeavor of coming to know mathematics.

Number Talks help students understand what, for many students, has been lost in the focus on division as a rote procedure. Through Number Talks, students can make sense of division (the operation—not the standard algorithm) and, by maintaining a focus on the relationships between quantities, learn how to size up a problem to determine a reasonable "ballpark" answer.

As with the other operations chapters, we examine efficient strategies for whole numbers, fractions, and decimals. Some of the strategies for division are different than the others in this book because in these, students may choose to keep track of their thinking with paper and pencil. Keeping track this way can help students use methods they understand to solve problems that are too big or complex to do entirely in their heads. Fosnot and Dolk (2001) describe this as "thinking *with* your head" as opposed to thinking "in" your head. We introduce a model for reasoning with larger numbers—called "Make a Tower"—that students rarely invent on their own. We ask them to try this out because it works efficiently for problems with large dividends and/or large divisors and reveals important mathematical relationships that we want them to understand.

Instead of using one example problem to demonstrate the various strategies for division, we have selected different problems to highlight various strategies because specific strategies work more efficiently with different kinds of problems.

Five Strategies for Division

Dividend ÷ Divisor = Quotient

1. Multiply Instead: 17 ÷ 3

"I know 3 times 5 is 15, so I have five groups of 3; then I have 2 left, so my answer is 5 remainder 2."

"I did it the same way and got 5 groups, but I said I have 2 left that won't make another group of 3, just 2 out of 3, so my answer is 5⅔."

2. Chunk Out: 643 ÷ 30

"I said 10 times 30 is 300, so 20 times 30 is 600, so I took 20 groups of 30 (or 600) from 643 and that left me with 43. I took out 1 more group of 30, and that left me with 13, so I added 20 [groups of 30] and 1 [group of 30] and got 21 groups of 30 with 13 left out of another group of 30. So my answer is 21¹³⁄₃₀."

$$643 \div 30$$

$$21\tfrac{13}{30}$$

$$30\overline{)643}$$
$$-600$$
$$\overline{43}$$
$$-30$$
$$\overline{13}$$

20 ∘∘• — *Twenty 30s is 600*

1 •∘∘ — *one 30 is 30*

∘∘∘∘∘ — *13 left out of a group of 30*

(Note: In recording this strategy, the quotient is determined by adding up the number of groups that have been subtracted and then writing that at the top, as shown.)

3. Make a Tower: 531 ÷ 13

"I started by making a tower of multiples of 13: 13, 26, 39, 52. I multiplied 52 by 10 and got 520, so I took 40 groups of 13, or 520, out and that left me with 11. So I had 40 groups of 13, with 11 left. So my answer is $40\tfrac{11}{13}$."

"Tower" of 13s

×40	520
×4	52
×3	39
×2	26
×1	13

$$531 \div 13$$

$$40\tfrac{11}{13}$$

$$13\overline{)531}$$
$$-520$$
$$\overline{11}$$

40

4. Halving and Halving: 128 ÷ 32

"I halved both numbers and changed the problem to 64 divided by 16; then I halved them both again and got 32 divided by 8; then I did it one more time and got 16 divided by 4. I knew there were four 4s in 16, so my answer is 4."

$$128 \div 32$$
$$= 64 \div 16$$
$$= 32 \div 8$$
$$= 16 \div 4$$
$$\boxed{4}$$

A Note About Symbols for Division

To help students flexibly interpret symbols for division, we like to inter-change the symbols in division Number Talks. Students are easily confused about what is being divided into what, so it is good to interchange the symbols and reinforce how each division expression would be read in words.

For example, think about how your students would interpret this problem:

$$3 \div 15$$

This is correctly read as "3 divided by 15," but students often interpret it as "3 into 15," because most of their experience as early learners is with the representation shown here:

$$3\overline{)15}$$

Depending on the experience of your students, it is also important to use the fraction bar to indicate division and pave the way for its almost exclu-sive use in algebra. So $^3/_{15}$ could be correctly read as "three-fifteenths" or "three divided by fifteen."

Developing Division Strategies in Depth

1. Multiply Instead:

Multiply Instead highlights the relationship between multiplication and division. This strategy can make division more accessible because it builds on relationships students already know.

How to choose problems that invite students to Multiply Instead:

We start by looking for problems where the dividend is a multiple of, or close to a multiple of, the divisor and also builds on multiplication facts that they are likely to know. We usually start with a few problems such as:

$$15 \div 3 \qquad 21 \div 5 \qquad 17 \div 3 \qquad 19 \div 6 \qquad 27 \div 4 \qquad 18 \div 4$$

Students then use this strategy for other one-digit and two-digit divisor problems such as:

$$50 \div 7 \qquad 154 \div 12 \qquad 84 \div 9 \qquad 66 \div 8 \qquad 60 \div 15 \qquad 29 \div 14$$

Questions that are useful for the strategy of Multiply Instead:
- Why did you multiply ___ by ___?
- What did you decide to do with the leftovers?
- Did anyone think about the leftovers in a different way?
- Why could it make sense to use multiplication to solve a division problem?

Multiply Instead is listed first here because it is a strategy that students use naturally when starting to think about what division means. But because it relies on multiples, this strategy is not efficient for solving decimal and fraction problems.

2. Chunk Out:

Chunk Out is another strategy that students tend to invent for themselves when given the opportunity to reason about division. It can be very helpful because students can take out "chunks" that are easy for them to think about, and then they are left with a smaller amount to figure out. For example, given the problem $276 \div 13$, a student can remove (or chunk out) twenty 13s (or 260), leaving 16, and then take out one more 13, for an answer of twenty-one groups of 13 with 3/13 left or 21 3/13. The Chunk Out strategy is very helpful when it comes to estimating the answer to a division problem.

$$276 \div 13$$

$$
\begin{array}{r}
21\frac{3}{13} \\
13\overline{)276} \\
-260 \quad | \quad 20 \\
\hline
16 \\
-13 \quad | \quad 1 \\
\hline
3
\end{array}
$$

How to select problems that invite students to use Chunk Out:
To encourage Chunk Out, we often start with single-digit divisors and dividends that are close to, but greater than, ten times the divisor. Problems like these can get you started:

$$32 \div 3 \qquad 43 \div 4 \qquad 87 \div 8 \qquad 76 \div 7 \qquad 53 \div 5 \qquad 97 \div 9$$

Once students are comfortable knowing that they can chunk out amounts while doing a division problem, they will use this strategy with larger division problems. To encourage this, we select problems where the dividend is close to a multiple of 10 times the divisor, like the following:

$$63 \div 20 \qquad 273 \div 13 \qquad 468 \div 40 \qquad 283 \div 14 \qquad 246 \div 12$$

This strategy works efficiently for any division problem, no matter how large. For example, given the problem $23,573 \div 21$, a student can chunk out one thousand 21s, or 21,000, leaving 2573, and can then chunk out one hundred 21s, or 2100, leaving 473. Then he or she can easily chunk out twenty 21s, or 420, leaving 53; then chunk out two 21s, leaving 11, for an answer of $1,122^{11}/_{21}$. Again, when solving large problems it is reasonable for students to keep track of their moves on paper.

$$23,573 \div 21$$

$$1 \ 122 \tfrac{11}{21} \text{ or } \approx 1,122 \tfrac{1}{2}$$

$$
\begin{array}{r}
21 \overline{) 23,573} \\
- 21,000 \quad | \ 1000 \\
\hline
2,573 \\
-2100 \quad | \ 100 \\
\hline
473 \\
-420 \quad | \ 20 \\
\hline
53 \\
-42 \quad | \ +2 \\
\hline
11 \quad | \ 1122 \tfrac{11}{21}
\end{array}
$$

Questions that can be useful for Chunk Out:
- How did you decide what chunk to take out?
- How did you keep track of what you had leftover?
- How did you decide what to chunk out next?

Chunk Out with Decimals

Chunk Out can quickly become cumbersome with decimals. But while it is not generally useful for precise answers, well-chosen problems can give students lots of great practice with thinking about place value relationships and with mentally multiplying by powers and multiples of 10.

To maximize the potential of this strategy and keep the calculations from getting too messy, we choose divisors with one decimal place and dividends comprising two- or three-digit whole numbers.

We were surprised at how interesting these problems can be, and we hope you'll explore them on your own, as we did.

Example Problem: 949 ÷ 8.5

"Ten times 8.5 is 85, so I took out one hundred 8.5s, or 850, leaving 99. Then I took out another ten 8.5s, or 85, and that left me with 14. Then I took out one more 8.5. So I used one hundred eleven 8.5s and had a remainder of 5.5, so I thought about my answer being about 111⅔. (For more about the dilemma of including a fraction when solving a decimal division problem, see the Halving and Halving strategy that follows.)

$$949 \div 8.5$$

$$
111\tfrac{5.5}{8.5} \text{ or} \approx 111\tfrac{2}{3}
$$

$$
\begin{array}{r}
8.5\overline{)949} \\
850 \quad | \quad 100 \\
\hline
99 \\
85 \quad | \quad 10 \\
\hline
14 \\
-8.5 \quad | \quad 1 \\
\hline
5.5
\end{array}
$$

Problems to get you started:

134 ÷ .5	56 ÷ .2	14 ÷ .3	18 ÷ .4

Problems to extend their learning:

13.7 ÷ .3	14.8 ÷ .4	3.75 ÷ .6	72.3 ÷ .7

(Note: We have found that Chunk Out, although interesting to play around with, is not efficient or useful with fractions.)

3. Make a Tower:

Make a Tower is a strategy that we have not seen students invent, but it can make many division problems much easier to solve when multiples of the divisor are not easy to find. You might want to share it with students as a strategy you tried or one that you got from someone else. This is a strategy that we first saw in the Investigations in Number, Data, and Space curriculum (Kliman et al. 1996), and one that we have seen students use with ease. For example, given the problem 529 ÷ 17, students make a "tower" of multiples of 17, or 17, 34, 51. With 51 they have three 17s, and if they multiply that by 10, they have thirty 17s or 510. They can take 510 from 529, leaving 19 and then take out one more 17, for an answer of 31²⁄₁₇.

$$529 \div 17$$

$$
\begin{array}{rl}
\times 30 & 510 \\
\times 3 & 51 \\
\times 2 & 34 \\
\times 1 & 17
\end{array}
\qquad
\begin{array}{r}
31\frac{2}{17} \\
17\overline{)529} \\
-510 \quad \big|\ 30 \\
\hline
19 \\
-17 \quad \big|\ 1 \\
\hline
2
\end{array}
$$

The "tower" is a column of multiples of the divisor. Students use the tower to decide what multiple of the divisor to subtract each time. Students can do this in many different ways; it is not important that they subtract the largest possible multiple each time. If we push students to always find the largest one, then the process becomes just another algorithm to try to follow. Students need to make sense of division in their own ways. See, for example, how another student did this problem:

"I started to make a tower of 17s: I did 17, 34, and then I realized that it was easy to do ten 17s, so I skipped to 170. Then I took out 170, and that left me with 359. Then I took out another 170 and another 170, and that left me with 19. Then I took out one more 17. So altogether I took out thirty-one 17s, and there were 2 left, so my answer is 31 2/17."

$$
\begin{array}{rl}
\times 10 & 170 \\
\times 2 & 34 \\
\times 1 & 17
\end{array}
\qquad
\begin{array}{r}
31\frac{2}{17} \\
17\overline{)529} \\
-170 \quad \big|\ 10 \\
\hline
359 \\
-170 \quad \big|\ 10 \\
\hline
189 \\
-170 \quad \big|\ 10 \\
\hline
19 \\
-17 \quad \big|\ 1 \\
\hline
2
\end{array}
$$

It often takes several tries for students to become more savvy about how to use the tower most efficiently.

How to select problems that invite students to Make a Tower:
To encourage students to use the Make a Tower strategy, we often select problems in which the dividend is close to multiples or powers of 10 of the divisor.

Problems to get you started:

  211 ÷ 7   186 ÷ 6   39 ÷ 12   410 ÷ 13   530 ÷ 17   271 ÷ 13

Once students have used the strategy of Make a Tower successfully, they will readily apply it to larger problems such as:

  856 ÷ 21   1815 ÷ 15   1920 ÷ 16   578 ÷ 23   5612 ÷ 17

Questions that can be useful with the Make a Tower strategy:
- How did you decide where to stop on your tower?
- How many ____ did you have when you stopped?
- Why do you now have ____ groups (of the divisor)?
- How many groups did you use altogether?

Make a Tower with Decimals

Make a Tower works the same with decimals as with whole numbers, but although it can be an efficient way to get a ballpark estimate of the quotient, subtracting groups of multiples often results in somewhat messy subtraction problems and remainders that can be difficult to determine.

Example Problem: 46 ÷ 2.03

"I made a tower of two multiples of 2.03: 2.03, 4.06. Then I multiplied 4.06 times 10, which gave me 20 groups of 2.03 or 40.6. I took that out of 46 and that left me with 5.4, so I took out 2 more groups of 2.03 or 4.06. That left me with 1.43 as a remainder. So my answer is 22 and a little more than ½."

$$46 \div 2.03$$

$$
\begin{array}{ll}
\times 20 & 40.6 \\
\times 2 & 4.06 \\
\times 1 & 2.03
\end{array}
$$

$$
22\,\tfrac{1.34}{2.03} \text{ or } \approx 22\tfrac{1}{2}
$$

$$
\begin{array}{r}
2.03\overline{\smash{)}46} \\
-40.6 \qquad \quad 20 \\
\hline
5.4 \\
-4.06 \qquad \quad 2 \\
\hline
1.34
\end{array}
$$

We haven't found this to be a useful strategy with fractional divisors, but you might find something we haven't thought of!

4. Halving and Halving:

Once students discover that with multiplication they can double one factor and halve the other, it is common for them to try to do the same with division and then wonder why their answers don't make sense. This is a perfect opportunity to turn a Number Talk into a lesson where students investigate why Halve and Double doesn't work with division (see Chapter 9).

A Note About Halving and Halving

Halving the divisor and the dividend can make many division problems easier to solve by changing a problem into an easier one. When this strategy is used, though, it is important to notice how the remainder changes. You will note that when halving both numbers, the remainder will be an equivalent fraction, but when using the term *remainder* in a nonfraction form, interpreting the remainder can be tricky.

Example: 58 ÷ 4

"I divided 58 and 4 by 2 and changed the problem to 29 ÷ 2. I know half of 28 is 14, and half of 2 is 1, so my answer is 14½."

$$58 \div 4$$
$$29 \div 2$$
$$14\tfrac{1}{2} \div 1$$

Note that 58 ÷ 4 is 14¾. The answers are both equivalent in this case. When using the term *remainder*, though, 58 ÷ 4 results in the answer 14 remainder 2, while 29 ÷ 2 results in the answer 14 remainder 1.

> When dividing numbers that are context-free, students should express remainders as fractions or decimal fractions. When a division problem is presented in a context, though, how you deal with remainders matters because the answer to a division problem can be different, depending on the context. For example, given the problem 13 ÷ 4, the answer can be 3, 3¼, 3.25, or 4, depending on the context. If 13 balloons are shared equally with 4 kids (13 ÷ 4), how many balloons will each child get? Three. If 13 brownies are shared equally among 4 kids, how many brownies will each get? 3¼. If $13 is shared equally among 4 kids, how much will each get? $3.25. If 13 students are going on a field trip and each car has room for 4 students, how many cars will be needed? 4. So technically the answer to a division problem should be "It depends on the context."

How to select problems that invite students to use the Halving and Halving strategy:
To encourage the use of Halving and Halving, we choose problems where both the divisor and the dividend are divisible by 2. We might start with problems like the following:

| 26 ÷ 4 | 52 ÷ 4 | 128 ÷ 8 | 192 ÷ 24 | 288 ÷ 16 | 46 ÷ 4 |

Do you think this strategy could be extended to numbers other than 2? For example, taking a third and taking a third? Investigate to find out. See the section "Will It Always Work? Investigation 5: Halving and Halving in Division" in Chapter 9.

Once students are aware that they can make problems easier, they often adopt this as their first approach for division problems, especially if the divisor is more than one digit. Problems such as these are good to try with your students:

| 364 ÷ 16 | 278 ÷ 12 | 1280 ÷ 24 | 1464 ÷ 28 | 321 ÷ 12 |

The Halving and Halving strategy can spark an interest in investigating the divisibility rules because students will now have an interest in quickly determining if any of the divisibility rules apply to the numbers they are working with.

Questions that can be useful with the strategy of Halving and Halving:

- How did you determine if both numbers were divisible by ___?
- How did this make the problem easier?
- How did you keep track of what you did?

Halving and Halving with Fractions and Decimals

Halving and Halving works with decimals just as it does with whole numbers, although in the Halving and Halving Investigation in Chapter 9, students will find that it is Doubling and Doubling that makes decimal problems easier. Also, multiplying both divisor and dividend by a power of ten is a lovely way for students to discover why the traditional algorithm works (but please don't tell your students this!).

Decimals Example Problem: 35 ÷ .5

"I multiplied both numbers by 2 and changed the problem to 70 divided by 1. So my answer is 70."

$$35 \div .5$$
$$70 \div 1$$
$$70$$

Example Problem: 2.6 ÷ .2

"I multiplied both numbers by 10, so my new problem is 26 ÷ 2. I knew there were 13 twos in 26, so my answer is 13."

$$2.6 \div .2$$
$$= 26 \div 2$$
$$= 13$$

Example Problem: 1.35 ÷ .03

"I multiplied both numbers by 100 and changed the problem to 135 ÷ 3. Then

I made a tower of 3s: 3, 6, 9, 12 and then multiplied 12 times 10, for 120. Then I took out 40 groups of 3, or 120, and that left me with 15. Then I took out 5 more groups of 3, so my answer is 45."

$$1.35 \div .03$$
$$= 135 \div 3$$

$$\times 40 \quad 120$$
$$\times 4 \quad 12$$
$$\times 3 \quad 9$$
$$\times 2 \quad 6$$
$$\times 1 \quad 3$$

$$\begin{array}{r} 45 \\ 3 \overline{)135} \\ -120 \\ \hline 15 \end{array} \bigg| 40$$

As seen in the preceding problems, the Halving and Halving strategy is wonderful for helping students understand how and why the decimal shifts places in division problems. But the strategy can also result in complicated reasoning if students are still expected to use the traditional algorithm for decimal long-division problems. Consider the following.

Example Problem: 13.57 ÷ .6

"I multiplied both numbers by 100, so my new problem is 1357 ÷ 60. I took out 20 groups of 60, or 1200, and had 157 left. Then I took out 2 groups of 60, or 120, and had 37 left, so my answer is $22\frac{37}{60}$ or just about $22\frac{2}{3}$."

$$13.57 \div .6$$
$$= 1357 \div 60$$

$$22\frac{37}{60} \approx 22\frac{2}{3}$$

$$\begin{array}{r} 60 \overline{)1357} \\ -1200 \\ \hline 157 \\ 120 \\ \hline 37 \end{array} \begin{array}{l} 20 \\ \\ 2 \end{array}$$

In the example above, the strategy is still a useful way to quickly determine a reasonable—rather than exact—answer. You'll decide whether it is problematic that the answer to a decimal division problem includes a fraction.

Halving and Halving works with fractions, too, because any fractional divisor can be changed into a whole number.

Example Problem: ⅓ ÷ ⅙

"I multiplied ⅙ by 6 to make the divisor 1; then I multiplied ⅓ by 6, so I had ⁶⁄₃ ÷ 1, for an answer of 2."

Example Problem : ½ ÷ ⅔

"I multiplied ⅔ by 3 to make the divisor ⁶⁄₃, or 2. Then I multiplied ½ by 3. So I had 3⁄2 ÷ 2 and my answer was ¾."

$$\times 3 \left(\begin{array}{c} \frac{1}{2} \div \frac{2}{3} \\ \downarrow \\ \frac{3}{2} \div \frac{6}{3} \end{array} \right) \times 3$$

$$= \frac{3}{2} \div 2$$

$$= \frac{3}{4}$$

or

"I multiplied ⅔ by 3⁄2 to make the divisor 1; then I multiplied ½ by 3⁄2, and my answer was ¾."

$$\times \frac{3}{2} \left(\begin{array}{c} \frac{1}{2} \div \frac{2}{3} \\ \downarrow \\ \frac{3}{4} \div 1 \end{array} \right) \times \frac{3}{2}$$

$$\frac{3}{4}$$

The Halving and Halving strategy is closely related to the Divide by One strategy that is an investigation in Chapter 9.

The various strategies for division of whole numbers, fractions, and decimals allow students to make sense of division and don't leave them stranded with only the traditional algorithm or a calculator to rely on. More importantly, Number Talks allow us to stay true to the message that everyone can make sense of mathematics—even division!

8

Making Sense of Fractions (and Decimals and Percent)

One day, as Cathy was working with sixth graders to help them find different ways to compare fractions, the class was unusually passive—and almost sullen. Finally she stopped and asked what was wrong. After a minute or so, Anthony spoke up, and, even though it was some years ago, his words are still etched in her mind: "Mrs. Humphreys, we had fractions in third grade and fourth grade and fifth grade. We didn't get them then, and we don't get them now—and we don't want to do them anymore!" Not being able to "get" fractions made Anthony feel unsuccessful—and who wants to work on things that make us feel like that?

But, for success in high school, there is no avoiding fractions. Students who are successfully learning complex concepts in algebra, trigonometry, and calculus can become confounded by a fraction in the middle of an equation. Katie, a junior in Cathy's Algebra 2 class, was outgoing and conscientious; she was taking both AP English and History and was active in student-body activities. But her confidence faltered when she walked into math class, and the sight of a fraction stopped her in her tracks. One day she called Cathy over to help her solve this equation:

$$0 = \left(\frac{3}{4}\right) \cdot 2 + b$$

Katie:	What does *that* [pointing at (¾) · 2] mean?
Cathy, thinking Katie was just confused about the notation:	"It means to multiply three-fourths by 2.
Katie:	I can't do fractions! Do I times 3 and 4 by 2?

Most middle and high school teachers have had similar experiences with their students. Without understanding fractional relationships, students have only their memories to fall back on, and, as Van de Walle and Lovin (2006) point out, "When mixed together, the myriad rules for fractions computation become a meaningless jumble" (88). Students' understanding of decimals and percent has met a similar fate; rules about moving decimal points—which ones to move, how many places, and which direction—become so muddled in many students' minds that the quantities involved are lost.

This chapter, therefore, has a different goal and structure than the chapters on whole-number operations. Because understanding fractional relationships supports understanding of both decimals and percent, we devote most of the chapter to ideas for supporting students' understanding of fractions. Then we look briefly at how some of those same ideas apply and extend to decimals. Finally, there is a short section on understanding percent and finding the percent of a number.

Thinking About Fractions

Our primary goal in the following Number Talks is to shore up the fragile understanding that most upper-grade students have about what fractions *mean*. Students whose experiences have been primarily procedural—which at this time means probably most of our students—have gotten into the habit of viewing a fraction as two unrelated numbers (the numerator and denominator) rather than as *one number*: a relationship between those two quantities. Katie, for example, didn't think about ¾ as a quantity that is a little less than 1; she saw the 3 and the 4 as discrete and unrelated numbers. This unfortunate tendency can be directly traced to the traditional algorithms for addition, subtraction, multiplication, and division of fractions that teach students to act on numerators and denominators separately. Therefore, the Number Talks in this chapter seek to help students develop a sense of quantity for fractions, decimals, and percent.

You will hear fewer student "voices" in this chapter, and, because students across the grades suffer from the same muddled thinking about fractions, we haven't done much in this chapter about "extending" thinking to more challenging problems. This chapter is for foundation-building; as always, you will be the best judge of which of these Number Talks will most benefit your students.

"More or Less?" Number Talks

In the "More or Less?" and "Closer To" Number Talks, we don't care about exact answers; our goal is to have students approximate the size of a fraction relative to the benchmarks of ½ and 1. We are also not looking here to develop sophisticated estimation strategies; rather, our focus is on helping students develop an intuition about fractions.

In "More or Less?," students decide whether a fraction is greater or less than ½. The following vignette shows how the Number Talk evolved in a seventh-grade class:

More or Less Than ½?

Mr. Jordan:	For this Number Talk, I am going to put a fraction on the board. When I do, I would like you to decide whether it is less than or greater than ½ and be ready to explain how you know.

Mr. Jordan writes ⅝ on the board. Students' thumbs come up almost immediately. When he asks for the answer, Megan says, "Greater."

Mr. Jordan:	Greater than what?
Megan:	Greater than ½.
Mr. Jordan:	Did anyone get a different answer? (No one.)
Mr. Jordan:	Who is willing to explain how you thought about this?
Andie:	4 is half of 8, and 5 is more than 4, so ⅝ is greater.
Mr. Jordan:	Why is 4 important in this problem?
Andie:	Because ⅘ is exactly ½, so ⅝ has to be more than ½.

Mr. Jordan, who could also ask for another student to explain Andie's thinking, decides instead to move on to another method.

| Mr. Jordan: | Who thought about this differently? |
| Sam: | I doubled 5—so 5 and 5 is 10, and 10 is greater than 8, so ⅝ has to be greater. |

Mr. Jordan now wanted students to articulate general ideas for quick ways to assess the size of a fraction.

| Mr. Jordan: | Can someone describe how Sam's method and Andie's methods are alike and different? (No one volunteers.) Talk to people around you; how did Sam and Andie think about it differently? |

When few students are willing to share with the whole class, Mr. Jordan often has students turn to one another in small groups.

| Liam: | I think Andie cut 8 in half to see what half of it would be, but Sam timesed [*sic*] 2 times 5. |
| Mr. Jordan: | Liam, are you saying that while Andie halved the denominator, Sam doubled the numerator? (Liam nods.) Okay, let's try this fraction (writes ⁵⁰⁄₉₉ on the board). Is this more or less than ½? |

When choosing problems for this activity, we look for fractions that are close to ½ with both even and odd denominators. We have found that larger numerators and denominators (such as ⁵⁰⁄₉₉) may help students focus on the quantities—and even get them more interested! You probably can do more than one of these per Number Talk.

Problems to get you started (adapted from Reys et al. 1987):

$$\frac{3}{8} \qquad \frac{16}{31} \qquad \frac{14}{25} \qquad \frac{50}{99} \qquad \frac{5}{9} \qquad \frac{8}{5} \qquad \frac{13}{23} \qquad \frac{24}{49}$$

Questions that are useful:

- Who can describe a method that would work for any fraction so that we could tell whether it was more or less than one-half?
- Who figured this out a different way?
- How are these methods alike and different?

(Note: Keeping a public, written record of these strategies can be helpful—even if some of them are flawed; doing so can help students learn to use language clearly and give the class something to refer to, or disagree with, in the future.)

"Closer to 0, Closer to ½, or Closer to 1?" Number Talks

In this activity that builds on "More or Less?," students consider the size of fractions relative to 0, ½, and 1 whole. At first, we look for fractions whose denominators are familiar to students or are close to denominators that are easily converted to decimals or percent.

Problems to get you started (adapted from Reys et al. 1987):

$$\frac{13}{24} \qquad \frac{16}{25} \qquad \frac{5}{16} \qquad \frac{3}{10} \qquad \frac{2}{5} \qquad \frac{10}{21}$$

As students become more confident, it is interesting to choose fractions that might cause a disagreement and unearth misconceptions, such as:

$$\frac{3}{17} \qquad \frac{6}{71} \qquad \frac{17}{24} \qquad \frac{31}{41}$$

And, to further increase the challenge, you might want to add ¼ and ¾ as benchmarks!

As students are learning to think about fractions as quantities, they have opportunities to explore Mathematical Practices that are also evident in the other Number Talks. They need, for example, to communicate their thinking clearly and make convincing arguments (MP3). Students don't always agree with one another's answers and/or reasoning on these problems, so this gives students an opportunity to learn how to settle a disagreement without turning to the teacher for the "right" answer. The following vignette shows how this happened in one class.

Is ⅔ Closer to 0, ½, or 1?

Prior to giving this problem, Ms. Lee's seventh-grade class had come to the general agreement—which she had not disavowed—that when the numerator and denominator are close together, the fraction is closer to 1.

JoAnne:	Closer to ½. (Lots of hands pop up immediately, and Ms. Lee asks them to put their hands down and put their thumbs up on their chests if they have a different answer to share.)
Ms. Lee:	Does anyone have a different answer?
Hugo:	Closer to 1.
Ms. Lee:	Does anyone think ⅔ is closer to 0? (No one.) Okay—we have two answers. That means we have mathematical disagreement! Who would like to defend one of the answers?
Cassie:	I think ⅔ is closer to 1 because 2 and 3 are close together, and last week that was one of the ways we thought we could tell.
Angel:	Yeah, but we also figured out that ¾ is exactly halfway between ½ and 1.
Ms. Lee:	Angel, how does ¾ help us with this problem?
Angel:	I think ⅔ is smaller than ¾, so . . . (His voice trails off.)
Ms. Lee:	Hmm. What do you think Angel is getting at? Talk to the people around you.

After students talk to one another for a while, Ms. Lee calls on Shawn.

Shawn:	Angel thinks ⅔ is less than ¾.
Ms. Lee:	Is that right, Angel? (He nods.) How would that help us figure out whether ⅔ is closer to ½ or closer to 1 whole?
Liam:	I just noticed something! In ½, 1 and 2 are close together, but ½ isn't closer to 1 whole because it *is* ½!

Ms. Lee, wanting to keep the focus on Angel's theory:
That's interesting, Liam! Hold that thought, and we will come back
to it in a minute. Let's go back to Angel's theory. Angel, how would
knowing that ⅔ is less than ¾ help us?

Angel: Well, ¾ is halfway between ½ and 1 . . . can I come up?

Ms. Lee: Sure. (Angel goes to the board and draws a line, marking
½ and 1. Then he puts ¾ between ½ and 1.)

**Angel, turning to Ms. Lee, who reminds him to turn to talk to the
whole class:** If ⅔ is less than ¾, then it has to be in here (pointing to
the segment of the line between ½ and ¾), and that means it has to be
closer to ½.

(Student muttering, "Oh, I get it.")

Ms. Lee: What do others think about this? (A few students nod,
but no one says anything else.)

Ms. Lee: Hmmm . . . who can say Angel's theory in their own
words?

Sarah: Angel might be saying that if ¾ is halfway between ½ and
1, and ⅔ is less than ¾, then ⅔ has to be closer to ½.

Ms. Lee: Is that right, Angel? (Angel nods.) You are using important mathematical thinking here. Mathematicians often
say, "If this is true, then that is true." So what Angel is
saying is, if ¾ is halfway between ½ and 1, and if ⅔ is
less than ¾, then ⅔ is closer to ½ because it is between
½ and ¾.

*Ms. Lee has revoiced Angel's idea because "if . . . then" thinking is so important in
mathematical reasoning. She writes Angel's thinking on the board:*

If $\frac{3}{4}$ is halfway between $\frac{1}{2}$ and 1,

and if $\frac{2}{3}$ is less than $\frac{3}{4}$,

then $\frac{2}{3}$ is closer to $\frac{1}{2}$ than it is to 1.

| Ms. Lee: | But I am wondering . . . how do we know *for sure* that ⅔ is less than ¾? Talk to people around you; how could you convince someone that ⅔ is less than ¾? |

Students talk in small groups for 3–4 minutes. Chris volunteers.

Chris:	Well, I changed ⅔ to %. And I knew ½ equals ⅜ and 1 whole equals %. And 4 is closer to 3 than it is to 6.
Ms. Lee:	So you are agreeing with Angel that ⅔ is closer to ½ but thinking about it in a different way than he did? Did anybody think of a different way to convince us that ⅔ is less than ¾?
Alicia:	Well, I didn't think of this until now, but you could change ¾ to ⁹⁄₁₂ and ⅔ to ⁸⁄₁₂. So ⁸⁄₁₂ is less than ⁹⁄₁₂.
Ms. Lee:	Before we stop, let's go back to what Liam noticed. What do we think about our conjecture that if the numerator is close to the denominator, the fraction will be closer to 1?

▍"Which Is Greater?" Number Talks

In this activity, we give students another kind of opportunity to reason about relative quantities. All students have been taught to find common denominators to compare fractions, and many also like to change fractions to decimals; still others have been taught to "cross-multiply" to see if two fractions are equivalent. But all students can compare fractions in ways that make sense to them, and offering opportunities to reason with these comparing problems helps them develop a greater depth of knowledge about fractions.

The following fractions help students develop more flexibility in comparing fractions because their denominators don't convert easily to decimals and percent. We often start these Number Talks by saying, "How could you figure out which fraction is greater *without* cross-multiplying or finding a common denominator?"

Example Problem: ³⁄₆ and ⁷⁄₁₅

Students might reason in these ways:

> "³⁄₆ is ½ and 7½ fifteenths would be ½, so ⁷⁄₁₅ is less than ½"
>
> Or, "3 and 3 is 6, so that's a half, but 7 and 7 is 14, so ¹⁴⁄₁₅ is less than a whole, so ⁷⁄₁₄ is less than ½"
>
> Or, "I'm wondering, could you do 6 times 2½ is 15, but 3 times 2½ is 7½, so it's not enough times to be the same? Does that work?"

Problems to get you started:

³⁄₆ and ⁷⁄₁₅	¹⁄₇ and ¹⁄₅	¹¹⁄₁₃ and ⁹⁄₁₁	³¹⁄₆₄ and ³⁷⁄₅₀
⁸⁄₃₅ and ¹⁵⁄₇₀	⁸⁄₉ and ¹⁰⁄₁₁	⁷⁄₁₁ and ⁷⁄₉	¹⁵⁄₃₈ and ⁵⁄₁₃

A couple of "thorny" problems to challenge your students:

⁴⁄₅ and ¹⁷⁄₂₄	³⁄₁₆ and ⁴⁄₂₁

▎"Fractions on the Number Line" Number Talks

(adapted from Burns 2007)

Students often think about fractions as parts of a whole but have less experience thinking about fractions as measures, or points on a number line. In this task, students order fractions on an open number line, focusing on relative, rather than exact, placement.

The teacher starts by drawing an open, or empty, number line on the board, marked only with 0, ½, and 1. The line extends in both directions from 0 and 1. Ahead of time, the teacher has written several fractions on sticky notes: ¾, ⁴⁄₅, ⁵⁄₆, ¹¹⁄₁₃, ⁹⁄₁₁, ⁷⁄₉, and ⁷⁄₁₁. The vignette that follows shows how this Number Talk unfolded with the first two fractions: ¾ and ⁴⁄₅.

Fractions on the Open Number Line

> **Ms. Laney, holding up the ¾ sticky note:** Who is willing to place ¾ on the number line?

Lisa volunteers and places it midway between ½ and 1.

> **Ms. Laney:** Let me know with your thumb if you agree with Lisa's placement. (All thumbs go up.)

Ms. Laney could have stopped at this point to ask Lisa how she knew, but Ms. Laney didn't want to take time away from the conversation about where the next sticky note would go.

Ms. Laney then holds up the ⅘ sticky note and asks students to think about where it would go on the number line.

> **Ms. Laney:** Is anyone willing to place ⅘ on the number line?

Justin walks up and places it to the right of ¾.

> **Ms. Laney:** Let me know with your thumb if you agree with this placement. (Lots of thumbs go up.) Justin, can you explain how you decided where to put ⅘?
>
> **Justin:** Yeah. I thought about ¾ as 75% and ⅘ as 80%, so ⅘ was a little bigger than ¾. (Ms. Laney records 75% above the ¾ on the number line and 80% above ⅘.)

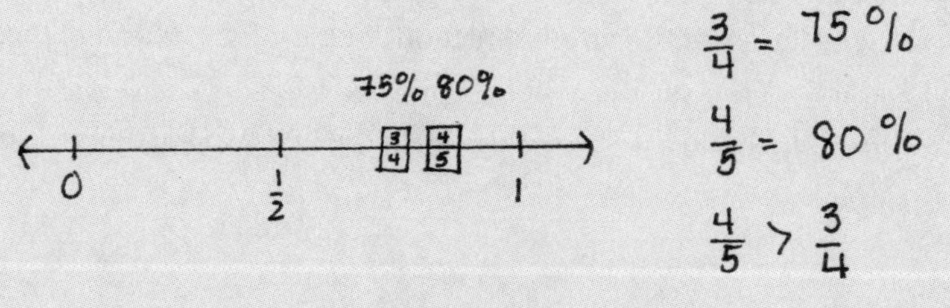

$$\frac{3}{4} = 75\%$$

$$\frac{4}{5} = 80\%$$

$$\frac{4}{5} > \frac{3}{4}$$

Ms. Laney:	Did anyone think about this differently?
Mariah:	I thought about ¾ as halfway between ½ and 1, and 2½ fifths would be a half. Half of 2½ fifths is 1¼ fifths. So 3¾ fifths would be halfway between ½ and 1; and 4 is bigger than 3¾, so ⁴/₅ is bigger than ¾.

This is a really interesting way to decide whether ⁴/₅ is more or less than ¾, but Ms. Laney chooses not to focus on it at this time. First of all, she had trouble herself trying to follow Mariah's logic. Also, she thinks this idea might not be accessible to all of her students—not to mention the time it would take to help everyone reason through it. But she does decide to make Mariah's thinking visually accessible.

Ms. Laney records 2½ fifths above ½ on the number line and 3¾ fifths above ¾ on the number line.

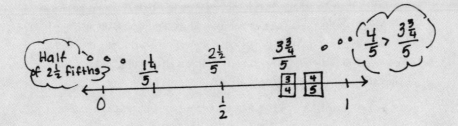

Ms. Laney:	Who thought about this differently?
Tennaye:	I thought ¾ is ¼ away from 1, and ⁴/₅ is ⅕ away from 1. Since ¼ is bigger than ⅕, ¾ is farther from 1 than ⁴/₅, so ⁴/₅ is bigger.

Ms. Laney and the class will continue working on this number line for a few days, using the other fractions on the sticky notes.

Activity 5: Approximating Sums and Differences

Students' Understanding of Addition of Fractions

In 1982, the National Assessment for Educational Progress (NAEP) gave this problem to 13- and 17-year-olds:

Estimate the answer to $^{12}/_{13} + ^{7}/_{8}$.

Students selected from one of four answers:

a. 1
b. 2
c. 19
d. 21

But only 24% of 13-year-olds were able to reason that the sum of a number a little less than 1 and another number a little less than 1 would be close to 2. This is about the same percentage you would expect, on average, if someone were to randomly draw one of four numbers out of a bag. Sadly, the 17-year-olds didn't do much better: far less than half (37%) were able to identify 2 as the best approximation.

In light of the continuing disputes about math performance and teaching in the United States, it is important to keep in mind that 1982 was the end of more than a decade of basic skills instruction. The NCTM *Curriculum and Evaluation Standards* (1989) had not yet been published, and the "math wars" were still in the future. While we don't know for sure, it is likely that students could have found common denominators and added the two fractions using paper and pencil. Nevertheless, the algorithm, even done correctly, does little good if students don't also have a sense of reasonableness of their answers. What good does an algorithm do if the answer is meaningless?

One thing is certain: teachers had been doing precisely what was expected of them. Many of us have been in this same position: feeling the frustration of teaching what is required and finding out later that at best it wasn't effective and at worst it caused all sorts of problems for kids. The way we were taught to teach fractions has particularly damaging fallout for kids. Many of us, for example, can hear ourselves in Van de Walle and Lovin's (2006) observation about "the myth of common denominators":

> Teachers commonly tell their students that to add or subtract fractions you must first get common denominators . . . [because] "after all, you can't add apples and oranges." This well-intentioned statement is essentially false. A correct statement might be "In order to use the *standard algorithm* to add or subtract fractions, you must first get common denominators." Using their own invented strategies, students will see that many correct solutions can be found without ever getting a common denominator. (90)

Therefore, in these next Number Talks, we focus on helping students learn how to determine which of two or three answers is *approximately* correct. In order to focus students' thinking on the quantities being added or subtracted—rather than on what *to do* to the numerators and denominators—we look for pairs of relatively unfriendly fractions that make finding a common denominator cumbersome.

Example Problem: $\frac{10}{41} + \frac{2}{11}$ **About ½   About 1   About 2**

A student with a good sense of fractions might say, "$\frac{10}{41}$ is close to $\frac{10}{40}$, so that's ¼. And $\frac{2}{11}$ is close to $\frac{2}{10}$, but that's $\frac{1}{5}$. And I know that ¼ plus ¼ is ½. But $\frac{1}{5}$ is close to ¼, so my answer is 'About ½'." Another student might say, "I know that ten–forty-firsts is about one-fourth and two-elevenths is less than two-tenths, so there's no way that they could add up to 1."

Yet another student might say, "Both of the fractions are way less than ½, so the answer can't be 1 or 2."

Problems to get you started (adapted from Lane County Mathematics Project 1983b):

$\frac{88}{91} + \frac{5}{6}$	About ½	About 1	About 2
$\frac{1}{7} + \frac{5}{16}$	About ½	About 1	About 2
$\frac{7}{8} + \frac{1}{9} + \frac{12}{13}$	About 1	About 2	About 3
$1\frac{1}{19} + 2\frac{17}{18}$	Less than 4	Greater than 4	
$5\frac{3}{4} - 2\frac{1}{5}$	Less than 3	Greater than 3	

▎Activity 6: Products and Quotients

Multiplication

Students' understanding of multiplication and division of fractions suffers from ailments similar to those of addition and subtraction. With multiplication, though, our initial goals are to help students think about the relationship between multiplication and division (for example, ¼ of something is the same as dividing that something by 4) and develop a sense of quantity when multiplying fractions. Following are several variations of Number Talks to help your students build stronger fractions sense.

Multiplying Fractions and Whole Numbers

Unlike the addition and subtraction Number Talks in the previous section, here we are looking for exact answers. In the first few problems we start with whole numbers times unit fractions (fractions with numerator 1). At first, we use unit fractions whose denominators are factors of the whole number, such as ⅓ of 12, ¼ of 100, and ⅕ of 20, to give us a sense of where students are. Even though many students think these are "easy," there are always others who don't yet have ways to access these problems. The beauty of Number Talks is that students who don't yet understand can learn by listening to the different methods of those who do.

One fifteen-minute Number Talk is probably enough time for several of these problems, but be careful to use them with a light touch; as soon as the problems become trivial, move to mixing in unit fractions whose denominators are not factors of the whole number. Students can often learn more from problems that stretch their thinking than from practicing problems that don't.

The work of Reys et al. (1987) and the Lane County Mathematics Project (1983) on estimation contributed many ideas to our thinking for the Number Talks that follow.

Example Problem: ¼ of 24

Some students will think about half of 24 to get 12, and half again to get 6, while others might count by 4s to get to 24. Others will divide 24 by 4. In each of these cases, even if they seem "obvious" to you, it's important to ask students why their thinking makes sense so that different approaches can become interrelated in students' minds.

Problems to get you started:

¼ of 32 **⅓ of 240** **⅛ of 56** **½ of 98** **⅕ of 350**

These unit fractions are building blocks for non-unit fractions. For example, ⅗ can be thought of as iterations of ⅕ (e.g., ⅗ = ⅕ + ⅕ + ⅕). "If ¼ of 36 is 9, then ¾ of 36 must be 9 + 9 + 9 (or 3 × 9) thirty-sixths, or 27/36.

Students, of course, will find different ways to think about these problems:

3/10 of 50 **⅔ of 27** **⅗ of 30** **¾ of 200** **⅝ of 16**

Then, if students can reason about ⅔ of 9, could they apply what they know to ⅔ of ⁹⁄₃₇? Or to ¾ of ¹²⁄₁₃? Or ⅗ of ²⁰⁄₂₁? (We hope you will play around with these ideas and perhaps even turn these problems into an investigation such as those in Chapter 9.)

▌"Messy" Fractions with Friendly Whole Numbers

Here, students turn messy fractions into friendlier ones in order to approximate the product. Again, the goal is to use numerical relationships flexibly to determine "about how big" a reasonable answer would be.

Example Problem: ⁸⁄₂₅ of 15 ≈

Students might reason in these ways (the more ways, the better!):

> "⁸⁄₂₅ is close to ⁸⁄₂₄, which is ⅓. And ⅓ of 15 is 5. So ⁸⁄₂₅ of 15 is close to 5."
>
> Or "I know ⁵⁄₂₅ is ⅕, and ⅕ of 15 is 3. And ³⁄₂₅ is a little more than half of ⁵⁄₂₅, so I think the answer is around 4½ or 5."

An interesting and mathematically fruitful follow-up question to this problem is "Would the answer be less than 5 or more than 5?" Questions like this can unearth even the most resilient misconceptions.

Students might reason that since 25 is greater than 24, then ⁸⁄₂₅ is greater than ⅓. Others might think the opposite. Once again, resist the urge to explain. For example, if Jennifer says ⁸⁄₂₅ is more than ⅓ because 25 is greater than 24, you could say, "So, Jennifer, it sounds like you are saying that if the denominator is larger (and the numerators are the same), then the fraction is larger." Turn the question back to the class: "What do others think about Jennifer's conjecture?" In the meantime, you can be thinking about another pair of fractions that would challenge Jennifer's thinking (such as ⅔ and ²⁄₉₉).

Problems to get you started:

¹⁵⁄₃₁ of 80 ≈	¹⁰⁄₉₉ of 60 ≈	¹²⁄₃₅ of 900 ≈
⁴⁰⁄₉₉ of 60 ≈	²⁴⁄₃₅ of 900 ≈	⁵¹⁄₆₁ of 600 ≈

Friendly Fractions with "Messy" Quantities

Problems where approximations are all that is needed occur regularly in life outside the math classroom. We start with numbers that are easy to round and fractions that students are familiar with.

Example Problem: ⅓ of 61

"61 is close to 60, and I know ⅓ of 60 is 20, so my answer will be just a little more than 20."

"I divided 61 into 3 groups, and that was 20, and I had 1 more, so I know it's 20⅓."

Problems to get you started:

$$½ \text{ of } \$29.95 \approx \qquad ¾ \text{ of } \$61 \approx \qquad ⅔ \text{ of } \$89.95 \approx$$

Approximating Multiplication of Fractions by Fractions

You can also challenge students with problems like this (adapted from Lane County Mathematics Project 1983b):

| $6⅜ \times 7\tfrac{9}{10}$ | Greater than 48 | Less than 48 |
| $1⅔ \times ¾$ | Greater than 1 | Less than 1 |

Division

The division of fractions algorithm is particularly baffling for students and teachers alike. Do you remember this ditty?

Yours is not to reason why;
just invert and multiply!

But without understanding what division means and why the algorithm works in the first place, students forget which fraction to invert. And with no sense of what the whole thing means, any answer is as good as another.

Chapter 9 includes two investigations that can help students make sense of division and even shed light on why invert-and-multiply works, but widespread access to calculators and computers makes it imperative that students develop a sense of the reasonableness of their answers. We can nurture sense-making about division through Number Talks.

We begin by focusing on having students reason about whether quotients are more or less than one whole.

> ## The Measurement Model for Division of Fractions
>
> Division of fractions problems can be interpreted in different ways; how they are interpreted depends largely on context. One interpretation is called the measurement (or "quotative") model. For division of whole numbers with this model, $15 \div 3$ asks, "How many sets of 3 (or how many 3s) are there in 15?"
>
> Similarly with fractions, $\frac{3}{4} \div \frac{1}{2}$ asks, "How many $\frac{1}{2}$s are there in $\frac{3}{4}$?" Interpreting these can be tricky, though, if the divisor is greater than the dividend. $\frac{1}{3} \div \frac{7}{8}$, for example, would read something like "How much of $\frac{7}{8}$ fits in $\frac{1}{3}$?" Thinking about division using the measurement model can help students consider *about how large* their answers should be. (For elaboration on models for division of fractions, see Ma [1999] and Fosnot and Dolk [2002].)

This example problem uses fractions that students can easily visualize, so they can get the idea of what is being asked. It also offers the opportunity to uncover misinterpretations of division symbols that students might have (see "Symbols for Division").

Example Problem: $\frac{1}{2} \div \frac{1}{4}$ Greater than 1   Less than 1

In $\frac{1}{2} \div \frac{1}{4}$, some students will think the quotient is greater than 1 (because $\frac{1}{4}$ is less than $\frac{1}{2}$), while others will think the quotient is less than 1—for the same reason! If this misconception arises, it might help to give students the problem $15 \div 3$ and ask them what the problem is asking. If they say, "How many times does 3 go into 15?," continue to ask, "How else can we explain what this problem is asking?" Then give them the problem $3 \div 15$ and ask, "What is this problem asking?" Understanding that when the divisor is larger than the dividend, the question shifts to "What part of 15 is in 3, or how much of 15 is in 3?" helps students better understand division of fractions.

Symbols for Division

The ÷ symbol, as noted in Chapter 7, is often read by students as "into" rather than as "divided by." This is exacerbated, or perhaps caused, by students' first introduction to division in problems like $3\overline{)45}$, which children read by saying, "3 goes into 45." Rather than clarifying this at the outset, we like to pose a division problem and have the issue arise in the discussion.

Problems to get you started (adapted from Lane County Mathematics Project 1983b):

⅓ ÷ ⅞	**Greater than 1**	**Less than 1**
2½ ÷ 1⅞	**Greater than 1**	**Less than 1**
1 ÷ ¾	**Greater than 1**	**Less than 1**
2⅞ ÷ 2½	**Greater than 1**	**Less than 1**

Reasoning About Division of Fractions

The problems in this section seek exact answers. Students who have developed a strong sense of reasonableness from the prior activities in this chapter will approach these problems flexibly.

Example problem: 1 ÷ ⅔

Students might reason like this:

- I know that a whole ⅔ goes into 1, and I know two ⅔ is too big to fit into 1, so I know the answer is between 1 and 2.
- There's one ⅔ in 1, with ⅓ leftover. ⅓ is half of ⅔, so my answer is 1½.
- I know ⅓ fits into 1 three times, so ⅔ could only fit into 1 half as many times. I think the answer is 1½.

An important question here is, "1½ what?" For an elaborated description and video of how this lesson unfolded in one seventh-grade class, see Boaler and Humphreys (2005, 40–53).

Problems to get you started (one Number Talk usually comprises 2–3 of these problems):

1 ÷ ⅓	3 ÷ ⅓	⅓ ÷ 3	⅔ ÷ ½	⅗ ÷ ¼
⅖ ÷ ⅓	⅖ ÷ ⅔	⅘ ÷ ¼	1 ¾ ÷ ½	1¾ ÷ 2

These problems are just the beginning; each Number Talk will help you to determine what problems to pursue next.

Thinking About Decimals

"More or Less?" Number Talks

In similar fashion to the fractions Number Talks, "More or Less?" Number Talks with decimals help students make sense of decimals by estimating to make comparisons. This helps students think about decimals as relationships based on place value.

For each operation, we choose combinations of numbers that are close enough to the answer to make them stop and think.

Problems to get you started (adapted from Lane County Mathematics Project [1983b]):

3.94 + 6.83	Less than 10	More than 10
15.8 + 13.89	Less than 30	More than 30
8.6 − 4.8	Less than 4	More than 4
3.8 − 1.86	Less than 2	More than 2
4.9 × 3.8	Less than 20	More than 20
9.91 × .9	Less than 10	More than 10
16 ÷ 1.9	Less than 8	More than 8

Problems to extend students' thinking:

Once students are comfortable with the boundaries offered by problems such as those above, they can begin problems such as this one from Van de Walle and Lovin (1988, 125):

> *Make an estimate and explain the way your estimate was made:*

73.46 + 6.2 + 0.582

"Where Is the Decimal Point?" Number Talks

In *Teaching Student-Centered Mathematics*, Van de Walle and Lovin (1988) pose fractions and decimals problems that fit nicely into a Number Talk structure. Consider, for example, the following two problems:

1. **Division** (p. 148):
   Put the following statement on the board or document camera and ask students to let you know with their thumbs when they know where the decimal place should go.

   146 ÷ 7 = 20857 is correct to five digits but without the decimal point.

   After collecting their answers, ask if anyone is willing to share how he or she thought about this, and of course, continue to ask if anyone thought about it differently. Then, uncovering each problem below, one at a time, ask students to use only the information above and estimation to give a "fairly precise" answer to each:

$$146 \div .07$$
$$1.46 \div 7$$
$$14.6 \div 0.7$$
$$1460 \div 70$$

   We have seen many students answer the initial question about placing the decimal point in 146 ÷ 7 accurately and give reasonable answers about why, and then blindly follow rules about moving decimals and give answers that make no sense at all to the follow-up questions. For example, they place the decimal point in the original problem after 20 and say something like, "There are 2 sevens in 14, so there are 20 sevens in 140, so the answer will be just a little more than 20, or 20.857." Many students then try to follow rules for moving decimals and move the decimal to the left (as it was in the divisor) and come up with an answer for 147 ÷ .07 of .20857. They don't stop to even consider that .07 is 100 times smaller than 7, so there will be 100 times more 7 hundredths in 147, not 100 times less.

2. **Multiplication** (p. 126):
   Have students compute the product of 24 × 63. They can use paper and pencil. Once the class has agreed on the answer, put the following on the board or document camera:

Using only the result of this computation and estimation, give the exact answer to each of the following:

$$0.24 \times 6.3$$
$$24 \times 0.63$$
$$2.4 \times 63$$
$$0.24 \times 0.63$$

You will want to use just one or two of these problems during a Number Talk, posing one problem at a time, giving students time to reason, collecting answers, and then listening to their different ways of thinking.

Once students have learned to reason with decimals, you will find that, as they are doing mathematics, many opportunities will arise where estimating with decimals would be helpful, and whenever this happens, you can take just a few minutes for a spontaneous Number Talk.

Thinking About Percent

In 1985, Ruth and Cathy were both teaching in California when the results of the new state assessment, CAP (California Assessment Program), were released. Across the state, middle-school teachers were stunned with the results on this eighth-grade question:

> *What is 100% of 32?*

Students were given these four choices:

    a. .32
    b. 32
    c. 132
    d. 3200

Only 50% of California eighth graders got the correct answer.

Four years later, on the 1986 NAEP, the following released item for 17-year-olds appeared in newspapers across the country:

> *Which of the following is true about 87% of 10?*

    a. It is greater than 10.
    b. It is less than 10.
    c. It is equal to 10.
    d. Can't tell.
    e. I don't know.

By now if you suspect the worst, you would be right. Only 51% of these high school students selected "It is less than 10."

Algorithms have an important place in mathematics and mathematics education, but they can't replace understanding important concepts. If middle and high school students come to us with the same gaping holes in their understanding as these eighth graders, then more practice with the same old rules for moving the decimal point won't help them build the foundations they need. The Number Talks that follow seek to shift students' thinking away from how to move the decimal point to what the quantities mean.

Activity 6: Representing Fractions as Percents

Number Talks, with a relatively small investment of class time, can provide an opportunity for students to become confident in their own reasoning about fractions and percent by using mathematical relationships that they understand. Students intuitively think more easily about percent than decimals, so we generally start there. To choose problems, we focus on fractions that are most commonly seen and used: halves, thirds, fourths, fifths, sixths, eighths, and maybe twelfths. Our goal is not for students to "memorize" these equivalencies but rather to reason through them by making sense of the relationships.

Example Problem: Writing ¾ as a percent

"I am going to write a fraction on the board. Without using a rule that you know, see if you can figure out how to represent or write it as a percent. Even if you know it 'by heart,' see if you could find a way to figure it out if you didn't know."

Possible ways students will think about this:

- I know ½ and ¼ make ¾; and I know ½ is 50%. And ¼ is half of ½, so half of 50% is 25%. So ¾ would be 50% plus 25%, so 75%.
- I know ¼ of a dollar is 25 cents, so ¼ equals 25%. And since ½ is 50%, 50% plus 25% is 75%.
- I thought about it like ____ did, but I just subtracted 25% from 100%.
- I know that 4 quarters make one dollar, and 3 quarters is 75 cents, so ¾ must equal 75%.

Problems to get you started:

$$\frac{7}{10} \qquad \frac{2}{5} \qquad \frac{1}{8} \qquad \frac{3}{8} \qquad \frac{5}{6} \qquad \frac{2}{3}$$

Problems to build on the reasoning they have developed:

$$\frac{3}{16} \qquad \frac{2}{25} \qquad \frac{5}{12} \qquad \frac{7}{20} \qquad \frac{3}{100}$$

Questions to support students' reasoning:

- How else could we figure this out?
- Why does your strategy/method make sense to you?
- Now that we have figured out _____, how could we use that to figure out _____? For example, now that we have figured out a percent for ⅙, how could we figure out ¹/₁₂? Or now that we have figured out ¾, how could we use that to figure out ⅜? Or now that we have figured out ⅛, how could we figure out ⅞?

Activity 7: Percent of a Number
(adapted from Lane County Mathematics Project [1983a])

Not only for success in school but as a life skill, students need to be able to calculate the percent of a number—or the approximate percent of a number—without picking up a calculator. For the following Number Talks, therefore, we focus on the percent of a number by building on students' generally strong understanding of 50%. This approach also helps students develop "if . . . then" reasoning; for example, if 25% of $400 is $100, then 12.5% of $400 has to be $50, because 12.5 is half of 25 and half of $100 is $50.

A goal in these problems is to help students learn to use what they know about one problem to help them figure out another. The need for this became clear to us when students in one high school class we visited had five different answers for 5% of 360°, even though they had just unanimously agreed that 10% of 360° is 36°.

Example Problem: 25% of $200
Students will reason about this in a variety of ways. Some will say, "I know 50% of $200 is $100. And I know 25% is half of 50%, so I need to find half of $100, which is $50." Or "I know 25% of $100 is $25, so 25% of $200 has to be twice that much, so that's how I got $50." Or "10% of $200 is $20, so 20% has to be $40. But 5% is half of 10% and half of $20 is $10, so $20 + $20 + $10 = $50."

One method, which a few students use naturally, is to find 1% of the number as a way to find any other percent. A student using this method might say, "I know 1% of $200 is $2, so 25% has to be 25 times 2, or $50."

The Download Progress Bar

From their experiences with Facebook, video streaming, and video games, most students are familiar with download progress bars. Since the progress bar often has a percent associated with it, this visual image is a good way for students to develop their percent sense. A similar model, called the "double number line," is also widely used as a way of representing ratios and rates.

   We will use 25% of $200 as an example of how you might use progress bars to support your students' understanding. We use the progress bar as a kind of double open number line, with only 0%, 50%, and 100% as benchmarks. The figure below shows a representation of 25% of $200:

The download bar can be used in a variety of ways. Some teachers use it to compare fractions and hours. Others give students progress bars (in progress) and have them figure out what percent is already downloaded.

Problems to get you started:

We offer only a few examples here because your choice of problems depends so heavily on what your students do with the initial problems. Each row below is based on the same quantity (in these examples, dollars and degrees). The arrows represent *possible* pathways for you to follow, depending on how your students are able to reason and not fall back on rote thinking.

50% of $200 → 25% of $200; then, you might try either 5% of $200 or 10% of $200 or 1%; or, if they know 50% and 25%, can they find 75%?

50% of 800 → 25% of 800 → 75% of 800 → and maybe try 10% now . . .

50% of 360° → 10% of 360° → 5% of 360° → 35% of 360°

A Note About 10%

We found out, from experience, that it may be best to hold off with 10% of a number for a while. 10% cries out for moving the decimal point and tends to pull students away from reasoning and draw them back into remembering.

Once students have become comfortable moving within a particular quantity, problems like this can be reasoned through in many ways. Just remember: we want to keep problems accessible so students can build their understanding and confidence.

85% of 60	12% of 60	37% of $500	45% of $300
250% of $800	2.5% of $100	20% of $350	45% of 150

Sometimes, students get more interested if the problems "look" really hard. Two high school teachers we know tried percents of fractions; they started with 200% of different fractions and then gave the students this: ¼ (200% of ⅗).

Percent *Of* Versus Percent *Off*

One high school class had just started doing Number Talks with percent of a number. In their first Number Talk, they found 50% of $200 easily, but when they were asked 25% of $200, there were three different answers: $50, $150, and $175. A student raised his hand and said, "How can 25% be more than half?" It took his wonderful question to unearth the confusion shared by many students, who were thinking that 25% of $200 meant 25% *off* (of) $200. This still doesn't explain $175 as an answer, but through probing, the teacher realized that the student had been thinking of $25, not 25%, off $200.

Students' errors often have underlying logic based on something they have learned, or think they have learned. That's another reason why Number Talks are such a great way to reveal misconceptions and misunderstandings that otherwise may never come to light.

As your students become stronger and you have a better understanding of what they can do, you can choose problems for Number Talks that are more and more complex—the fractions less friendly, the decimals more tricky, and the percents more complicated. Upper-grade mathematics content is full of fractions, decimals, and percents, and you only need to be alert to the possibilities and ready, at the drop of a hat, to take a quick fifteen-minute detour.

9

Number Talks Can Spark Investigations

Mathematics has the potential to amaze. We notice things that seem magical, and we can't help but wonder, "Why is this happening? How does this work?" And when we wonder, we want to find out. So we investigate. And that's what this chapter is all about. During Number Talks, there will be many times when you and your students wonder why something works, or if it will always work. When this happens, you have a perfect opportunity to turn Number Talks into an investigation. These investigations are likely to reveal important mathematical ideas. When you pose the question "Will it always work?," you open the door for students to examine the mathematics behind the various strategies from different perspectives, and there will be opportunities for students to see connections between seemingly unrelated mathematical ideas and between numbers, algebra, and geometry. The idea that students are pursuing a mathematical question that they have is, in itself, wonderful.

Investigations are a special kind of mathematical problem solving. They cultivate the natural inclination of young minds to ask "Why?" and "What can I find out about this?" And, of course, there is more than one answer, or discovery, and more than one way of getting there. Investigations offer the gift of time for those most basic of mathematical pursuits: tinkering with ideas, sniffing around for patterns, and making conjectures and testing them out. As we discuss in more depth at the end of the chapter, investigations, in embodying the Standards for Mathematical Practice, help students experience what mathematics is really all about.

For an investigation to realize its potential, we (as teachers) need to let go of our investment in how students approach their questions or what they find out. Hints that guide students down a particular path, for example, take away students' opportunities to find their own ways through a problem. This means that engaging students in investigations will take a little courage and some (possibly a lot of) perseverance on your part as students learn, maybe for the first time, how to pursue their own mathematical ideas—and you learn how to let them.

Investigations take time—class time. They don't have to be lengthy or complex, but you will find that they are well worth the time—and are experiences of which no student should be deprived.

Many investigations arise from particular strategies used in Number Talks and give students the opportunity to think about why a strategy works. The eight investigations in this chapter—one for addition, two each for subtraction and multiplication, and three for division—have the same primary purpose: to help students realize that when something happens over and over again in mathematics, *there has to be a reason*. So what is that reason? And will that something *always* happen? Why? Could I prove it? If not, when will it happen and when won't it? We call these "Will It Always Work? And Why?" investigations.

For each investigation, we suggest materials to have available, ways to pose the problem, and some of the mathematical ideas you will encounter. We also include comments about important mathematics to highlight in the investigations as well as misconceptions to be dispelled. Different components of the general investigation outline have been included for the various investigations. We have tried to highlight parts of each that will help you prepare.

Although we were tempted to included teacher–student dialogue along with the conclusions students draw from each investigation, we have purposefully not done so because we didn't want to deprive you and your students of the opportunity to make your own discoveries. We also didn't want to encourage you to look for a specific conclusion or answer. We know from experience that these investigations are accessible to students and that the discoveries that they (and you) will make along the way will take Number Talks to an even deeper level and will richly enhance everyone's understanding of how numbers work.

So, have fun with the ideas. And remember: one of our hardest jobs is to pose the problem, get out of the way, stay out of the way, and trust that our students will make sense of the investigations we pose.

What follows is a general outline of how a typical "Will It Always Work?" investigation unfolds.

I. Before the Investigation

Do the investigation yourself (you don't want to miss out)! Then try to anticipate all the ways students might approach it. Even when you do so, students are likely to surprise you with their ideas. Embrace this when it happens, and anticipate that you and your students will learn together during these investigations.

II. Posing the Investigation

Students often don't "discover" the strategies in these investigations, so you will need to introduce them. If you have short math periods, some of these investigations might take more than one day. Here is an example of how this might look:

1. *Do a Number Talk* as you normally would. After students have explained their strategies (and assuming no one has used this strategy), tell students you want to share a strategy that you saw in _____'s class or that you saw someone do. If, on the other hand, one of your students (Jason) has tried the strategy on his own, then tell students you want to examine Jason's strategy.

2. *Show the strategy*. Ask students to talk with a partner to see if they can figure out what the person had done; then share out. Students will probably have different ways of thinking about it.

> ### Teaching Tip
>
> One way to do this is to have them pretend they are describing this strategy—in words—to someone in another class.

3. *Students need to know what they are investigating*, so give another problem and have everyone try Jason's strategy with paper and pencil. Have a student come up and demonstrate "how Jason would do this problem."

4. *Teach the students how to "tinker" by saying*, "With a partner, make up three other problems and try them out using Jason's strategy." Emphasize the importance of keeping track—in a hopefully organized way—of their findings. Then, after a little while, "What did you find out?" Share out a bit.

5. *Teach students to wonder* by modeling: "Hmmm ... there has to be a reason why this keeps happening over and over again. Does anybody have a theory about why this works?"

A Note About Helping Students Notice and Wonder Why

Students who have been taught to mimic procedures often don't think to wonder, "Why . . . ?" Many years ago, Mary Baratta-Lorton observed, "A child who expects things to 'make sense' looks for the sense in things. A child who does not see patterns often does not expect things to make sense and sees all events as discrete, separate, and unrelated" (quoted in Burns 1984, 98). Once students begin to expect math to make sense, noticing and wondering why become the norm—and the world of mathematics opens up for them.

---

6. Now for the *homework:* "Will Jason's strategy *always* work? Be prepared to bring your thinking to class tomorrow. Your group will try to come up with a mathematically convincing argument for whatever answer you decide on."

A Note About Homework

"Think about" homework is uncommon but can be a valuable break from normal homework. While this is not an essential step, it does give all students time to think about the question before they work with others on a problem. We usually ask students to come in with some evidence of their thinking so that they have something to contribute to their group discussion. Some students may come back to class with mathematically sophisticated methods they have gotten from their parents; this is fine, as long as the student can explain why the method *makes sense.* If they can't (yet), then the method can be something for students to keep thinking about. On the other hand, some students might come with nothing on their papers, but they will still be part of hearing ideas that other students bring to the discussion, and over time they will begin to contribute.

III. Small-Group Work

Have appropriate manipulatives and grid paper available:

1. *Re-posing the problem:* "Can someone remind us of the problem we were working on last night?" (Hopefully one of them will remember!)

> There are a variety of models for small-group work, and you will find the way that works for you. We typically have students work in randomly formed groups of four for investigations but sometimes use smaller groups or partners.

2. *Small-group directions:* Write these directions (or something close) on the whiteboard or document camera:
   - Take turns sharing what you found out in your homework last night.
   - See if you can come to agreement on whether Jason's method will always work.
   - Figure out a way to convince us.

> ## A Note About Proof and Counterexamples
>
> Even young children can learn to make a general argument (for an elaborated discussion, see Carpenter, Franke, and Levi 2003, 85–103). Here are two ideas to get your students started:
>
> - If students use multiple examples to "prove" that a theory works, you might try asking, "But how do you know *for sure* that there isn't some problem way out there that this doesn't work for?"
> - Counterexamples are powerful. Students get excited to realize that all they have to do to disprove a theory is to find *one case* for which it does not work.
>
> Also: When students explain their thinking in your class, you and your students are building a *socio-mathematical norm* on what "counts" as a mathematical explanation. In some classes, for example, telling *how* they did a problem is sufficient. The Standards for Mathematical Practice emphasize that students need to be able to "construct viable arguments and critique the reasoning of others" (MP3). We frequently ask the class, "Do you think that was a mathematically convincing argument? Why or why not?" You will work out for your own class what it means to justify a mathematical argument.

3. Make your best guess about *how long students will have to work,* and make sure they know. Time limits are never right for everyone in a class. (We usually find that we underestimated.)

4. *While the students are working,* the teacher's job is to observe what groups are doing. Are students approaching it in similar ways? Are there approaches that might benefit from being shared back-to-back because they build on one another? Are there unusual approaches? Try to stay long enough at one table to be able to get the gist of where the group is going with their arguments. Listen, ask a probing question where necessary, but please do not succumb to the temptation to give "hints"! This is their problem to fiddle with; if you guide them too much, you rob them of their developing sense of agency and their aha! moments. Often students don't think to keep track of their ideas in ways that allow them to analyze and learn from the things they try. As students are working, you might have to encourage them to keep track, but try hard not to show them how to do this.

5. *Questions you can ask to develop the inner skeptic in your students:* Students have been so conditioned for quick conclusions that they often convince themselves that something is true before they have considered alternatives. They often don't think, for example, to test other *kinds* of numbers. It's good to keep an eye out for this and ask questions like "Will that work with negative numbers?" or "Have you tried it with fractions?" or "What about zero?"

We also want students to be skeptical enough not to be satisfied with one kind of justification so that they automatically push themselves to see how else they could prove something is true. We might ask, "Have you tried to represent it geometrically (or algebraically)?" or "How could you convince a skeptic?" Finally, if a group thinks they are done but the class as a whole is not ready for a discussion, you can ask this group, "Can you make up some problems on your own that might challenge the rest of us?"

A Note About Stamina

It is important for students to learn that they won't figure things out right away. Students aren't used to figuring things out for themselves, so they need to practice, just as a muscle is strengthened by gradually increasing weight. We have found that a frank conversation about how this feels followed by a brainstorming session about what things they can do when they are "stuck" can help. As they do more investigations, their stamina will improve, as will their tolerance for not knowing exactly what to do. The same thing is true for us—we have to develop the stamina to let our students have the time they need.

It takes a while to get the idea of what justifying is and what it isn't. By the time they get to middle school, many students completely accept the word of an "outside authority" (Hiebert et al. 1997) as a proxy for justification. In contrast, a central message in the Common Core State Standards is that students need to learn that one of their (new) main jobs in math is to assess the validity of claims for themselves through sense-making, constructing viable mathematical arguments, and critiquing the reasoning of others.

IV. Whole-Group Processing

Whole-group processing is for building mathematical knowledge. As students or groups of students share what they have discovered, others will have opportunities to look at ideas that they might not have previously considered. You'll want to ask the class to look for relationships between the different models they have used. It is during the sharing out of groups' findings that everyone has an opportunity to deepen their understanding of the mathematics involved. And groups of students who might not have delved very deeply into their own investigation have an opportunity to consider that they might have done more on their own.

A Note About the Order in Which Students Should Share

There are differing opinions on how to decide which groups share first, second, . . . and last. Different approaches are based on different philosophies and priorities, and different approaches have their own pros and cons.

Currently, deciding the order of sharing based on the sophistication of strategies, from least to most, is a popular notion. Using this method, it is argued, allows the underlying mathematical concept to build. We have valiantly tried this approach at one time or another but generally take a more organic approach. We walk around watching and listening and occasionally asking questions. Sometimes when we see a method that is unusual or highlights a mathematical idea or representation we want everyone to see, we quietly ask the students if they are willing to share. If they are reluctant, we sometimes ask if they are willing to let us share their idea, and they usually are.

Our colleague Patty Lofgren addresses an important synergy that happens when students are the ones to determine when they want to share:

No matter how many times I give kids a rich problem, I always see new ways of approaching the problem that just surprise the heck out of me. For any given group of kids, it is presumptuous to think I know what might resonate for students and cause them to say, "Oh, I see from Whitney's method why _____ worked, and I wonder if…." Those connections happen within students at their own place and time, and we learn a great deal from hearing those connections as they happen. Preselecting an order for sharing or scaffolding toward our "best explanation" can take the agency right out of the hands of students and make processing time almost algorithmic. (Personal communication)

During processing, there may be times you'll want to explain something yourself. In general we want to discourage this, but nothing bad will happen if you do this once in a while. It's just important that you don't expect that just because something is clear to you, you can pass on your clarity to someone else. Students are used to listening to their teachers' explanations, and saying something once won't hurt—as long as you don't expect the students to understand just because you have explained it. They need to make sense of ideas for themselves.

V. Wrap-Up

Once ideas or findings from an investigation have been shared, ask the class (or groups) to summarize the big ideas they have learned. As they share out, you can record these ideas on the whiteboard or ask students to record them in their math journals. Taking time to reflect on our learning is an important disposition we want students to develop.

The Investigations

"Will It Always Work? And Why?" Investigations

- Subtraction: Same Difference
- Addition: Swap the Digits
- Multiplying Fractions: Swap the Numerators or Denominators

- Multiplication: Halving and Doubling
- Division: Halving and Halving

Other Investigations

- Division: Divide by One
- Multiplication: Representing multiplication geometrically
- Subtraction: Do the same subtraction strategies that work for whole numbers also work efficiently for decimals and fractions?

Will It Always Work? Investigation 1: "Same Difference" in Subtraction

Example Problem: 63 − 29

"I made the 29 into 30 and the 63 into 64, so I changed the problem to 64 − 30; my answer was 34."

You will need: graph paper, color tiles or paper squares, rulers, scissors.

Following the general protocol for investigations described, let students know that this is an investigation of the Same Difference strategy (described in Chapter 4), and that their job will be to investigate whether this strategy will always work, and why or why not.

II. Posing the Investigation

Do a Number Talk using the problem 73 − 28. Record student solutions. If no one uses the Same Difference strategy of changing the problem to 75 − 30, then share that "some people solve the problem this way" and record as follows:

$$+2 \left(\begin{array}{c} 73 - 28 \\ 75 - 30 \end{array} \right) +2$$

$$45$$

Ask students to talk with others around them about how this student solved the problem and why they think it works. Ask them to try the strategy with three other problems of their choice, and then work together to see if they can figure out if the strategy will always work and why or why not.

III. Small-Group Work

As groups are working, circulate and observe their work. When appropriate, you can throw out a question like one of these and walk away, leaving them to ponder what you have asked:

- Can you also subtract the same quantity from both numbers?
- Does this strategy work for addition?
- Will it work with decimals? Fractions?

IV. Whole-Group Processing

Invite students or a group of students to come to the document camera and share their work and findings. You will want to remind the class that they have an important job as the group is sharing. They need to try to understand the ideas being shared, and if they can't understand something their job is to think of a question for the group that might help them understand. Remind them that you will ask others to build on the ideas being shared and to share other discoveries that their groups made.

Sometimes when a group is sharing, others start talking within their groups. Sometimes this is because something being shared has triggered an idea their group was working on or now understands. If this is the case, you'll want to ask the presenter to pause, and provide some time for groups to talk together about an idea. Other times, students might just not be paying attention. And when this happens we usually say, "_____, could you please wait until others can hear you?" Continue to ask others to share their group's findings.

Mathematical approaches we have seen from students:

- Some students make a number line and cut out a strip of paper of a particular length and then slide the strip up and down the number line, showing that changing the numbers, whether adding or subtracting, doesn't change the distance between the two numbers. (Note: This is an example of using a particular case—the length of the paper strip—to demonstrate a general principle. An even more general argument would be if we were to imagine the strip as being elastic and that it could stretch or shrink to any length.)
- Other students make two rows of color tiles to represent the two numbers. They note the difference between the two numbers, then add the same number to each row and check that the difference is still the same. They demonstrate this several times. (Note that this again is a particular case [the number of tiles] to represent a general principle.)
- Students who have had algebra *may* (but it is just as likely that they won't!) use algebraic notation to prove the general case:

$$a - b = (a + \mathbf{c}) - (b + \mathbf{c})$$
$$= a + c - b - c$$
$$= a - b + c - c$$
$$= a - b$$

If algebra is the only method that students use for a convincing argument, push them to come up with a visual or geometric representation to support their algebraic argument. Also, if you have been learning about the properties of arithmetic operations, you might ask students to identify the properties that support each algebraic move they made.

V. Wrap-Up

Ask students, either in their groups or together as a whole class, to identify the "big ideas" they discovered during the investigation. Again, you might want to record these ideas on chart paper or have students record them in their math journals.

Will It Always Work? Investigation 2: Swap the Digits in Addition

You need: plain paper. Place value blocks are useful but not essential for this investigation.

Example Problem: 93 + 29

"I swapped the digits in the ones place and changed the problem to 99 + 23, and that was 122."

It is not likely that your students will invent the Swap the Digits strategy on their own (but it will be exciting if they do!). It can be a very efficient strategy for certain problems. And the investigation of this strategy can help students better understand place value and the operation of addition.

II. Posing the Investigation

Do a Number Talk using the problem 93 + 29, and record student solution strategies. If no one uses the Swap the Digits strategy, introduce it as something you have seen. By swapping the digits, you can turn the problem into 99 + 23.

$$93 + 29$$
$$= 93 + 29$$
$$= 99 + 23$$
$$99 + 1 = 100$$
$$+ 22$$
$$\overline{122}$$

Ask students to talk to people around them about what they think this person did.

Follow the general outline for investigations described by having students try the strategy with another problem like 29 + 91. Then pose the problem "Will Swap the Digits always work? Why or why not?"

III. Small-Group Work

Questions you might want to ask while students are working:

- Which digits can you swap and which can't you swap?
- Does Swap the Digits work with subtraction? Why or why not?
- What about multiplication?

Even young students will make important mathematical discoveries about place value and addition while investigating this strategy. Enjoy!

Will It Always Work? Investigation 3: Swap the Numerators or Denominators in Multiplying Fractions

Example Problem: $\frac{5}{6} \times \frac{6}{7}$

"I swapped the numerators and made the problem $\frac{6}{6} \times \frac{5}{7}$. That's the same as $1 \times \frac{5}{7}$, so my answer is $\frac{5}{7}$."

You will need paper and graph paper.

II. Posing the Investigation

Because students and teachers might not be familiar with this strategy, we have included a vignette from a Number Talk that Ruth recently did with a group of teachers.

Ruth asked the teachers to figure out the answer to $\frac{6}{7} \times \frac{2}{3}$ without using a rule that they know. Here is what happened:

Ruth:	I'm going to write a problem on the document camera, and I want you to figure out an answer without using a rule that you already know.

Ruth writes $\frac{6}{7} \times \frac{2}{3}$ on the document camera and waits until thumbs are up.

Ruth:	Who is willing to share how you made sense of this problem?
Maria:	I divided $6/7$ into three groups, so I had $2/7 + 2/7 + 2/7$. I took two of those groups and that was $4/7$.
Matthew:	Why did you use two of the groups?
Maria:	Because $2/3$ means two out of three, so I took two out of the three groups of $2/7$.
Matthew:	Oh, I get it!
Ruth:	Does anyone else have a question for Maria? (No one does.) Who thought of it differently?
Justin:	I knew I needed $2/3$ of six of something. While I was thinking about it, it didn't really matter what the something was. I knew $2/3$ of six is 4, so I had 4 somethings and the somethings I had were sevenths. So my answer is $4/7$.

Ruth waits to see if anyone asks a question of Justin. No one does, and Ruth asks a question herself.

Ruth:	Justin, you said you needed $2/3$ of six something. Could you explain a bit more about what you meant by that?
Justin:	Well, if I needed $2/3$ of $6, I would need $4. Or if I needed $2/3$ of six basketball players, I would need 4 basketball players because $2/3$ of six is 4. So I just thought about I needed $2/3$ of six, or four. Then I said, well, I want $2/3$ of $6/7$, so the six something is sevenths, so $2/3$ of $6/7$ is $4/7$.

Ruth waits to see if anyone has another question for Justin. No one does.

Ruth:	Does anyone have another way to think about it?
Hannah:	I thought about it like Maria, but Bill has a neat way.
Ruth:	Bill, are you willing to share your way, or would you rather have Hannah share it?
Bill:	I swapped the denominators, so I changed $2/3$ times $6/7$ to $6/3$ times $2/7$. $6/3$ is 2, so I did 2 times $2/7$, and I got $4/7$.

$$\frac{6}{7} \times \frac{2}{3}$$

$$= \frac{6}{3} \times \frac{2}{7}$$

$$= 2 \times \frac{2}{7}$$

$$= \frac{4}{7}$$

Ezra:	Wow! Can you do that?
Ruth:	That's a good question, Ezra. I think we should try to find out. Would you take a minute to talk in your small groups about what Bill did?

After giving teachers a couple of minutes to talk about Bill's strategy, she asked them to explain what they think Bill did. Then she asked them to try Bill's strategy with the problem ⅔ × ⅗. (Take a moment to think about this yourself.)

After having teachers explain what Bill might have done with this new problem, Ruth told them that they were going to investigate if Bill's strategy of Swap the Numerators and Denominators will always work and why. She asked them to begin their investigation by thinking about the following problems:

$$\frac{2}{5} \times \frac{3}{4} \qquad \frac{3}{7} \times \frac{2}{6} \qquad \frac{5}{9} \times \frac{3}{5} \qquad \frac{4}{7} \times \frac{1}{2} \qquad \frac{6}{7} \times \frac{2}{3}$$

As participants worked together, Ruth circulated, checking in with groups to see what they were thinking along the way. As they struggled to figure out when and why Bill's method works, Ruth encouraged them to represent the problems geometrically to see if that would help. She also encouraged them to try the strategy with mixed numbers, and to keep track of their trials and findings as they worked in order to figure out when the strategy works efficiently.

IV. Whole-Group Processing

- During whole-group processing, press on what students have discovered about when swapping digits works efficiently and when it doesn't, and the relationships between the numerators and denominators that make it an efficient strategy.
- This is also an opportunity to examine the commutative property of multiplication at work.

Will It Always Work? Investigation 4: Halving and Doubling in Multiplication

Example Problem: 8 × 13

"I halved the 8 and doubled the 13, so I changed the problem to 4 times 26; then I did 4 times 25 is 100, and 4 times 1 is 4. So my answer is 104."

$$8 \times 13$$
$$= 4 \times 26$$
$$= 4 \times (25+1)$$
$$4 \times 25 = 100$$
$$4 \times 1 = \underline{+4}$$
$$104$$

You will need: graph paper, color tiles or squares of paper, scissors.

This investigation explores the Halving and Doubling strategy for multiplication in Chapter 5.

II. Posing the Investigation

Begin with a Number Talk for the problem 8 × 27, and then follow the general overview for investigations described. When you ask students to investigate the strategy, you might suggest that they begin with examples with small factors, such as 4 × 6 or 3 × 6. Once they can demonstrate the strategy with small numbers, ask them to try it with other numbers and be prepared to share their findings with the class.

III. Small-Group Work

Questions to pose during small-group work include the following:
- Will it only work with even numbers?
- What would happen if, instead of halving, you took a third of one factor?
- Can you represent this strategy geometrically?
- What generalizations can you make?
- Would this work for division?

This last question can lead to "Will It Always Work?" Investigation #5.

IV. Whole-Group Processing

Mathematical arguments we have seen from students:

- Some students have set up a rectangle with color tiles to represent a multiplication problem—let's say 4 × 6. They then halve the dimension of 4, and slide the last 2 rows up to the top, leaving a 2 × 12 rectangle. They then explore the idea with different-sized rectangles.

- Other students have used graph paper. They draw a variety of rectangles and show how half the rectangle is moved to the other dimension, resulting in the halving of one dimension (one factor) and doubling of the other.

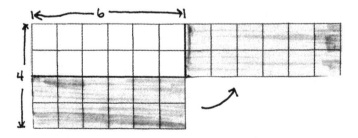

(Both of these strategies, again, are particular cases. To move students toward generalization, you can ask, "How do you know for sure that there isn't some rectangle out there that this doesn't work for?")

- Some groups might use the associative property of multiplication to explain what is happening in a special case:

$$4 \times 6 = (2 \times 2) \times 6 = 2 \times (2 \times 6)$$

- Other groups have used algebra as in the following approach; as with the subtraction investigation, it is good to have the students identify which property they used at each step along the way.

$$ab = \left(\frac{1}{2} \cdot 2 \right) \cdot ab$$

$$= \frac{1}{2} (2a) b$$

$$= \frac{1}{2} (a \cdot 2) b$$

$$= \left(\frac{1}{2} a \right) (2b)$$

- Some students, after we have wondered aloud whether this strategy would hold for numbers besides 2 (Halving and Doubling), have expressed a more generalized version that can lead to an algebraic representation of the identity and inverse properties of multiplication such as the following:

$$ab = \left(\frac{1}{c} \cdot c \right) a \cdot b$$

$$= \frac{1}{c} (ca) \cdot b$$

$$= \frac{1}{c} (ac) \cdot b$$

$$= \left(\frac{1}{c} \cdot a \right) (cb)$$

Generally, we ask students who have approached these problems using algebra to see if they can represent the situation geometrically. It is powerful when students learn that geometry can be used to illuminate algebraic relationships, just as algebra can be used to generalize geometric relationships. And it is sad that algebra and geometry are learned as separate topics in the United States. In most other countries, including those that perform at the top on international studies, algebra and geometry are taught in integrated courses.

Will It Always Work? Investigation 5: Halving and Halving in Division

Example Problem: 26 ÷ 4

"I changed the problem to 13 ÷ 2. Since 6 times 2 is 12, my answer is 6½."

You will need: graph paper and scissors. Color tiles or paper squares are useful but not necessary for this investigation.

When students learn the Halving and Doubling strategy for multiplication, they often want to use it not only for multiplication but also for division. When this happens, it is best to resist giving an explanation and instead just express interest that it doesn't seem to work and wonder why not. This is a great opportunity for students to investigate their own questions.

II. Posing the Investigation

Begin with a Number Talk using the problem 48 ÷ 16. Record students' different ways of solving the problem. If no one uses the Halving and Halving strategy, share the strategy with the class and record as follows:

$$48 \div 16$$
$$24 \div 8$$
$$\boxed{3}$$

Pose another problem (42 ÷ 12), and ask them to try the Halving and Halving strategy.

Tell students that they will be investigating if the strategy of Halving and Halving will always work with division. Ask them to try the strategy with three more division problems, and then work together with their groups to figure out whether the strategy will always work for division, and why.

III. Small-Group Work

Questions you might ask during small-group work:

- Did you try to double and double? Does that work?
- Will the strategy work for numbers other than 2 (for example, taking a third and a third, etc.)?
- Will it work with decimals?
- What generalizations can you make?
- Can you represent the strategy geometrically?
- What does the remainder mean when it changes? Do you really get the same answer?

- Why do you halve and double with multiplication and halve and halve when dividing?
- What's the same and what's different about multiplication and division?
- Have you tried halving and halving with fractions and decimals?

As outlined in Chapter 7, understanding that the Halving and Halving strategy combined with the Divide by One strategy that follows can make many division of decimal problems much easier to solve.

While the remaining investigations in this chapter are not "Will It Always Work?" investigations, they follow the same general structure. The difference is that there is one specific outcome or goal for each of these investigations.

Investigation 6: Divide by One

Since it is not a strategy that we have seen students invent for themselves, this is a strategy that you might want to share with your students (see Chapter 2).

II. Posing the Investigation

Begin this investigation by writing the following problems one at a time on the board and asking, "What is ___ divided by one?" or "What is ___ times 1?"

$3 \div 1$ $17 \div 1$ $44 \div 1$ $6 \div 1$ $9 \div 1$ 23×1 7×1

At this point you might want to introduce 1 as the multiplicative identity (because any number multiplied or divided by one is equal to the number itself).

Say, "So if we can easily change a division problem into one where the divisor is 1, we've got a simple problem to solve. I'm going to put some problems up, and I want you to see if you can change them into division problems with a divisor of 1."

Put the following problems on the document camera.

$68 \div 2$ $110 \div 5$ $39 \div 3$ $224 \div 2$ $150 \div 5$ $336 \div 3$

Ask students to share how they changed each problem to get a divisor of 1.

Next we ask them to investigate if Divide by One works with division of fractions and decimals. In order to get students to explore this, we sometimes do a Number Talk where we pose a division of fractions problem in a form they are not used to seeing, for example:

$$\frac{1}{2} \overline{\smash{)}\ \frac{2}{3}}$$

Since students are not used to seeing division of fractions in this format, they often have a difficult time thinking about the problem. Having memorized the "invert and multiply" rule doesn't help them because when the problem is posed this way, they have a hard time remembering which number to invert. If you pose the problem above, and have students mentally find an answer, you will likely be surprised by how many different answers they suggest. Some students mistakenly think the question is asking for ½ of ⅔ and suggest the answer ⅓. Others invert the wrong number and end up with the answer ¾. Still others think the question is asking for ⅔ of ½, for an answer of ²⁄₆.

This might be a good time to ask the questions "Will the Divide by One strategy help us here?" and "What would we have to multiply ½ by to make it 1?" These two questions can launch an investigation of what number you can multiply a fraction by to get 1. In the process of answering these questions, students will be exploring the inverse property of multiplication, an idea that is important when it comes to solving algebraic equations.

Next, write ⅔ ÷ ⅓ on the board. Ask students to change the problem to an equivalent problem where the divisor is 1. Say, "Give everyone a chance to think about this on their own, then when your group is ready, talk together about what you did." Then ask for a volunteer who will come to the document camera and show what he or she did.

Next, write the following problems on the document camera, and ask students to work together to change each problem to an equivalent problem where the divisor is 1, and tell them that their job is then to investigate if Divide by One will always work with fractions and decimals, and why.

⅖ ÷ ⅕   ¾ ÷ ¼   ¾ ÷ ⅛   ⅔ ÷ ⅓   ⁴⁄₃ ÷ ⅔   ⅖ ÷ ⅖

V. Wrap-Up

Important mathematical ideas:

- Divide by One is based on the fact that 1 is the multiplicative identify; that is, every number multiplied or divided by 1 is equal to the number itself. So if we can easily multiply or divide a divisor to get it to 1, we can simplify any division problem. For example, given the problem 3 ÷ ⅓, we can multiply both the dividend and the divisor by 3 making the problem 9 ÷ 1, for an answer of 9.
- Divide by One builds on Halving and Halving and can help us understand why the mysterious "invert and multiply" rule works. Here we use the example ⅔ ÷ ¾.

$$\frac{2}{3} \div \frac{3}{4}$$

want this expression to be equal to 1

$$\Rightarrow \left(\frac{2}{3} \times \underline{\quad}\right) \div \left(\frac{3}{4} \times \underline{\quad}\right)$$

$$\Rightarrow \left(\frac{2}{3} \times \underline{\quad}\right) \div \left(\frac{3}{4} \times \frac{4}{3}\right)$$

But these two have to be the same.

$$\Rightarrow \left(\frac{2}{3} \times \frac{4}{3}\right) \div 1$$

$$\Rightarrow \frac{2}{3} \times \frac{4}{3}$$

The division of fractions algorithm is a good example of how, in the service of efficiency, the meaning and complexity of its underlying steps are hidden. As Bass (2003) says, "If we wanted a machine to solve such a class of problems, the algorithm would tell us how to program the steps that the machine should perform on any instance of the problem to get the desired answer" (323). But our students are not machines. Young minds crave meaning, and depriving them of the chance to make sense extinguishes their natural desire to know why things work.

Investigation 7: Geometric Representations in Multiplication

You will need: plain paper (not graph paper).

Investigating the Break a Factor into Two or More Addends strategy provides an opportunity to help students make sense of important mathematical relationships by using geometric representations to make connections among arithmetic, geometry, and algebra. Because there is a specific outcome we are aiming for in this investigation, we have included a more complete description of how this investigation might unfold.

II. Posing the Investigation

Pose the challenge by saying something like "We're going to investigate ways of representing the Break a Factor into Addends strategy geometrically. First I'd like you to think about the problem 8 × 13. Let me know when you have had enough time to solve it mentally." You can be fairly certain that someone will break the 13 into (10 + 3) and then multiply 8 × 10 and 8 × 3. Let's call this person "Janet" and record her thinking as follows:

$$8 \times 13$$

Janet $\quad 8 \times (10+3)$

$$8 \times 10 = 80$$

$$8 \times 3 = \underline{24}$$

$$104$$

Say, "I want you to think about how you might represent Janet's way of solving the problem geometrically. This may be new to many of you, so please give everyone time to think about it on their own. As soon as everyone in your group is ready, take some time to share your different ideas about how to represent this geometrically." Anticipate that some students won't know what you mean by "geometric," so let them puzzle over this in their small groups (if you are tempted to draw an example, students will want to mimic what you do). If students haven't started talking together after a few minutes, remind them that they should share their ways of representing this in their small groups.

Then invite students to come to the document camera to share their ways of recording the problem geometrically. Don't be surprised if students have ways of doing this that you have not anticipated, or that are not efficient, and maybe that don't make sense to you or don't seem "correct." For example, we have often had students draw 13 rows with 8 circles in each row. Although this was not what we had in mind—and won't be effective with large numbers or fractional dimensions—their method is a visual representation of 8 × 13. "Where is the 8? Where is the 10? The 3?" are all good questions to ask.

If no one has used the geometric representation below, ask, "If I were to draw a rectangle that represents 8 × 13, who could tell me how to draw it?" (without drawing it themselves—this gives students experience with describing dimensions).

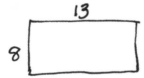

"Okay, what does the 104 have to do with this rectangle?" (area)

Then, "Think for a minute. How would we make this rectangle represent the way Janet thought about 8 × 13?" (We would probably have them talk in their groups about this.)

Then, "Who could describe how Janet's method would look in this rectangle?"

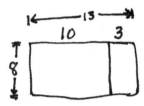

Then, "Where would the (8 × 10) be in this rectangle? The (8 × 3)?"

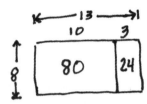

If someone has used this representation, dig into it as above. You also might choose, depending on the experience of your students, to connect the geometric representation of Janet's method with a more formal numerical representation and connect the two representations to each other.

$$8 \times 13$$

$$8 \times (10 + 3)$$

$$(8 \times 10) + (8 \times 3)$$

$$80 + 24$$

A Note About Geometric Representations

As you are drawing the rectangles, make the lengths represented roughly proportional. Don't worry about being precise. But in a two-digit-by-two-digit multiplication problem, it's best *not to* divide a square into four equal parts and fill in each part with a partial product, as drawn here.

$$12 \times 14$$

	10	4
10	100	40
2	20	8

> We're concerned that this practice can become more of a tool for get-ting answers than a model for understanding relationships. For example, we want students to connect 10^2 with its geometric meaning of "square."
>
> It is also very important that we not jump into four partitions unless we are representing the thinking of a student who has broken each factor into two addends. Some students will do 16 × 12, for example, as 16 × (10 + 2), which would result in only two partitions. This representation is just as good as partitioning into four parts.

Next, give a problem such as 12 × 16 as a Number Talk. On the board (or chart paper), record the different ways that students solved the problem. Hopefully you will have at least three or four solution strategies. *Be sure to record each way of solving the problem on chart paper or a whiteboard so students can refer back to them during their investigation.* If no one solves the problem by changing 12 to (10 + 2) and/or 16 to (15 + 1), then share that you have seen students solve it this way.

Ask students to work together to use a rectangle to solve the problem geometrically. Wander and observe as they are working together. If no one uses a rectangle to represent the solution, when you call the group back together, mention that you saw a lot of interesting ways to represent the problem and that we want to explore how a rectangle can be used to represent each solution strategy. Draw a rectangle on the document camera that is roughly 12 by 16. Ask, "Where would the 12 go on this rectangle?" "Where would the 16 go?" Next ask, "What did ___ do with the 12?" Divide the length of 12 on the rectangle into 10 and 2, trying to keep them roughly proportional. Ask, "What did ___ do with the 16?" Divide the length of 16 into 15 and 1. Ask students what number would go in each region of the rectangle, then add the amounts to find the product of 12 × 16. You will now have a rectangle that looks like this:

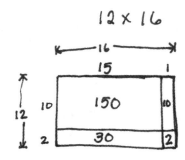

Another student might solve the problem by thinking about 12 × 16 as 12 × (12 + 4). In this case, the rectangle would look like this:

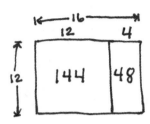

We use plain paper rather than graph paper for this investigation in order to encourage students to think about the area of the various regions involved. Graph paper tends to cause students to spend time figuring out the exact sizes and often results in counting rather than thinking about the multiplication involved.

III. Small-Group Work

Tell students they will be working to see if they can use rectangles to represent each of the other strategies that were shared during the 12 × 16 Number Talk. Ask them to give everyone some time to think on his or her own, and when their small group is ready, share their ways of recording with their group. (Note: Not all strategies can be represented with rectangles, but please don't tell your students! Let them bump into this themselves and try to figure out why.) Circulate and watch as groups are working. If your class didn't initially come up with very many strategies, encourage the group to come up with as many ways as they can think of to solve 12 × 16 using rectangles.

Let them know that when they are done, they should raise their hands, and you will give them a challenge. For the challenge, ask students to work in their groups to think of at least two different ways to solve the problem 26 × 48 and represent those two ways geometrically. They also can make up multiplication problems and solve these other problems on their own until they feel they can use geometric representations to solve multiplication problems with ease. For some students, using a geometric model becomes their favorite way to solve multidigit multiplication problems.

This geometric representation of multiplication lays an important foundation for multiplication of algebraic expressions. With algebra students, you can extend this investigation by asking, "How would you represent $(x + 1)(x + 2)$ geometrically?" and repeat the process described above. Share the following with your students in the same manner as you used with numbers above. As you do, ask students what the dimensions of the rectangle would be [$(x + 1)$ and $(x + 2)$].

$$(x+1)(x+2)$$

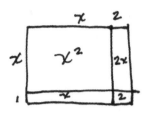

As you record, make sure that the two x's are roughly the same size (because, of course, both x's are the same number) and that $+2$ is roughly twice as long as $+1$. As you are drawing, ask students if they can see the $(x + 1)$ and the $(x + 2)$. Again, ask them to fill in the amounts in each interior rectangle. Then ask them to collect like terms by asking, "How many x^2's do we have? How many x's? What else?" After doing this, ask if someone is willing to come up and show how we usually solve this algebraically.

$$(x + 1)(x + 2)$$
$$x^2 + 2x + x + 2$$
$$x^2 + 3x + 2$$

Questions about where the terms of the algebraic expression show up in the geometric representation will help students connect the two representations, and in this way deepen and broaden their understanding of symbolic notation. It is also interesting to many students that x^2 is read "x squared" because a rectangle with the same length on each side is a square.

Following are several algebraic multiplication problems that students can explore. Be sure to ask them to represent each one geometrically. Should a question come up about how to represent a binomial with subtraction, we hope you will resist the urge to explain and, instead, put that question right back to them and see how they make sense of it.

$$(2x + 1)(x + 2) \qquad (2x + 1)(3x + 3) \qquad (x + 2)(x - 1) \qquad (x - 1)(x - 2)$$

I. Summarizing Efficient Strategies for Each Operation

When you are ready to move to another operation with whole numbers, be that addition, subtraction, multiplication, or division, you will want to ask students to work in their small groups to identify the few most efficient strategies they have been using and to name each strategy. After giving small groups time to work together on this, record each strategy they suggest on chart paper and ask the class what they want to name each strategy.

Once you have done this summary of efficient strategies for the operation, you are ready to pose an investigation on whether the efficient strategies that work for whole numbers also work for fractions and decimals. What follows is a description of how these investigations might unfold. We have used strategies for subtraction to illustrate a process you might want to use with each operation.

Investigation 8: "Play Around" with Subtraction Strategies

You will need: one "Strategies for Subtraction" handout for every two students (Appendix C) and one "Play Around with These" handout for each student (Appendix C).

Once you have done many subtraction Number Talks with whole numbers, you have an opportunity for a wonderful investigation with middle and high school students when you ask the question, "Will these same subtraction strategies work with fractions and decimals? Or with positive and negative numbers?"

II. Posing the Investigation

Pose the question, "Do subtraction strategies for whole numbers work for all rational numbers?" Give students the subtraction strategies handout.

- Adding up (represent with and without the open number line)

- Breaking apart the subtrahend (represent with and without the open number line)

- Adding the same quantity to the subtrahend and the minuend (represent with and without the open number line)

- Rounding the subtrahend to the nearest multiple of 10 (or 100, 1000, etc.) and compensating

- Using negative numbers

Write $61 - 27$ on the board or document camera. Then, for each strategy listed on the Subtraction Strategies handout, ask for volunteers to explain how the strategy would work for the problem $61 - 27$.

Next, give students the "Play Around with These" handout. Ask them to give everyone some time to think on their own, and when their group is ready, their job is to see if the strategies that work for subtraction of whole numbers also work for decimals and fractions.

$7.46 - 6.85$	$60.12 - 0.2$
$8.2 - .97$	$3\frac{1}{4} - 1\frac{5}{8}$
$3\frac{1}{5} - 2\frac{4}{5}$	$-5 - (-9)$
$-3 - 2$	

After a few minutes, encourage students to talk together as they work on the problems. Wander and observe as groups are working. When appropriate, ask if they are trying multiple strategies on each problem. When they are working with the negative numbers, probe to see how they know if the answer will be positive or negative. If groups don't do so on their own, nudge them to try the Same Difference strategy with negative numbers.

You might want to spend some time on these over a couple of days rather than have students finish their explorations in one setting. When groups have had enough time to explore, call the class back together. It is not important that everyone has explored every problem. Ask, "Are there any problems you want to be sure we talk about?" Expect that they will want to talk about the negative numbers problems. Let them know that you will be talking about those problems but that you don't want to start there.

When processing, begin by asking, "Which strategies did you tend to use most?" And then, "Were there any kinds of problems that called out for a different strategy?"

Work through each problem as a class, asking if students will share strategies they found particularly efficient for the problem. Be sure to ask each time if anyone used a different efficient strategy.

For the subtracting decimals and fractions problems, if no one used the Add Instead or the Same Difference strategy, ask them to do so, and ask for volunteers who are willing to come to the document camera and share how they did this.

Add Instead and Same Difference with Fractions and Decimals

When we first tried these problems ourselves using Same Difference and Add Instead, we couldn't help but wish we could have all our past students back whom we had taught to just line up the decimals and subtract. Of course we, like you, had seen many students who struggled to line up the decimals correctly, and students who when asked to order decimals thought .205 was larger than .41. We know now that the traditional algorithm allowed students to follow a procedure with little or no attention to the value of the digits. And once again we were surprised to find that Add Instead and Same Difference kept students focused on the value of the digits, while giving them an easy way to subtract both decimals and fractions.

When talking about the subtraction problems with negative numbers using a number line, you will want to note that although the distance between the numbers is always positive, the answers to the problems are not. Ask students how they were able to figure out if the answer was positive or negative. Probe to hear other explanations that students came up with for this.

Investigations and the Standards for Mathematical Practice:

These investigations bring nearly all of the Mathematical Practices to the foreground of instruction: make sense of problems and persevere in solving them (MP1); reason abstractly and quantitatively (MP2); construct viable arguments and critique the reasoning of others (MP3); attend to precision (MP6); look for and make sense of structure (MP7); look for and express regularity in repeated reasoning (MP8). As they take place in classrooms, these investigations build students' disposition to "do" and "see" mathematics, and they bring the Mathematical Practices to life.

In summary, you will find that Number Talks are rich with opportunities for authentic investigations. Nearly anytime you or your students ask "Will that always work?" or "Why?," you have the potential for a mathematical investigation sparked by a Number Talk. The investigation of questions like "Why can you divide a factor into 2 or more addends and distribute them across the other factor?" (for example, $12 \times 16 = (10 + 2) \times 16$) or "Why do you move the decimal place one place to the left when doing 10% of a number?" or "Why does the cross multiplication algorithm work?" or "Why can you swap digits with the same place value when adding two numbers?" can result in students having a robust understanding of operations and how they work on numbers in general and how they work on numbers between 0 and 1.

When we recognize the mathematics potential in student questions and honor their questions by providing the time to investigate, then students become creators as well as consumers of the curriculum.

We have long been inspired by and grateful for the words and wisdom of Eleanor Duckworth (1987) in "The Having of Wonderful Ideas." She writes:

> The wonderful ideas that I refer to need not necessarily look wonderful to the outside world. I see no difference in kind between wonderful ideas that many other people have already had, and wonderful ideas that nobody has yet happened upon. . . . The more we help children to have their wonderful ideas and to feel good about themselves for having them, the more likely it is that they will someday happen upon wonderful ideas that no one else has happened upon before. (14)

We trust that as you pursue these investigations with your students, there will be many, many opportunities to marvel at their wonderful ideas.

10 Managing Bumps in the Road

Although Number Talks are a short daily routine, there is nothing routine about them. At first, they appear to be deceptively easy . . . all we have to do is put a problem on the board and ask students how they got the answer, right? But every Number Talk takes on a life of its own when students start to explain their reasoning, and there is no road map for us to follow. We need to think on our feet about what to ask and how to respond. We need to consider who is talking, who isn't, what and how to write on the board—and we need to keep all of these things in our head at once. It is no wonder that it can be hard to know what to do next and easy to feel like we are spinning our wheels and getting nowhere.

These rough spots on the road to successful Number Talks may make it tempting to abandon the whole idea, but please don't—you *can* do this! And, as you will find, any difficulties that present themselves during Number Talks offer important learning opportunities for you and your students.

The following questions and answers address thorny issues that we and many other teachers have encountered over the years. For each question, we discuss strategies that we have found to be helpful in nudging students forward. Some strategies might work in one class but not in another; some Ruth has used with success, while others Cathy has found to be helpful. We also include "temptations to resist"—common teaching strategies we have found to be counterproductive.

Good teachers can make very different decisions—just as in mathematical problem solving, you may need to fiddle around with Number Talks until you find what works best for you and your students. We hope these ideas will help you persevere in the face of the challenges that are a natural part of learning.

Q: *What if I don't understand what a student is saying?*

A: This is an important issue for all of your students. If one student's explanation is hard for you to understand, other students probably don't understand it, either. And, since your ultimate goal is for students to listen to and respond directly to one another, it is important that all students learn to communicate clearly about mathematics so they can understand one another. This does not happen overnight. Before the adoption of the *Common Core State Standards for Mathematical Practice* (NGA/CCSSO 2010), for example, most students did not have regular opportunities to express their reasoning or present a mathematical justification. It is understandable that they would have a hard time expressing their ideas clearly during initial Number Talks.

When you find yourself in the position of not understanding what a student is saying, keep asking and rephrasing to see if you have interpreted their words correctly. You might say something like "Let me see if I really understand what you're saying. I think you. . . ."

Strategies That Have Worked for Us
- Ask, "What I think I heard you saying was _____. *Is that what you are saying?*" Just be careful to express what you actually heard them say.
- Ask, "I want to make sure I understand what you mean. Could you please repeat that last part?"
- Ask, "Who can explain what _____ said in your own words?"

Finally, if the preceding strategies haven't helped you, you can say, "I need some more time to think about your strategy, and I'll get back to you." Then do think about it and do talk to the student. In giving yourself time to think about an idea, you are also giving the student time to think about how they might express the idea more effectively. This way, you don't have to feel nervous about not understanding what is being said, and you won't have to worry about losing other students who can't follow a cumbersome or inarticulately expressed idea or procedure.

Temptations to Resist
Putting words into a student's mouth or assuming you know what a student is trying to say. This is so easy to do, especially when you are feeling the pressure of time. Keep probing the student's thinking and make it clear that it is *you* who does not understand—not that the student is doing a poor job of explaining. This will give the student confidence that his or her ideas are important to you.

Q: *How can I get my students to move beyond the traditional algorithm when solving a problem?*

A: A belief that there is one best way to solve a math problem is the tradition in the United States. Even though the *Standards for Mathematical Practice* state that students should understand the meaning of quantities and not just how to compute them, the transition between knowing "what to do" and understanding "why" takes a while. This is another reason why Number Talks can be such an important learning experience—even for high school students. Coming to know that there are many ways to solve nearly any problem is ultimately liberating to students and adults alike. Understanding numbers and how operations act on those numbers is foundational to the work that high school students do in mathematics. But empowering children to reason with numbers, rather than remember what they are "supposed" to do, takes time, patience, and grit.

Strategies That Have Worked for Us

- The first time the traditional US paper and pencil algorithm is offered as a strategy during a Number Talk, we explain briefly what an algorithm is.[1] From then on, whenever the so-called "regular" way arises as a strategy, we write *traditional algorithm* on the board. As the numbers get larger in Number Talks, students who continue to cling to these algorithms will gradually realize for themselves that other methods can be much easier and more efficient.

- We also try to find problems that are unwieldy with the traditional algorithm but easier using a different method; sometimes it takes a few tries before we find one that works. In one high school class, for example, after five unsuccessful attempts by the teacher to get students to reason in new ways, the students finally gave up the traditional algorithm when their teacher gave them this problem: "You are going to buy five milkshakes for you and your friends. Each milkshake costs $1.99. How much did you pay for the milkshakes?"

- Sometimes we say, "Someone in _____'s class did it like this. See if you can understand what they did." Then we choose another problem that lends itself to this new strategy so that students have a chance to try on the idea. First, ask students to share how they solved this next problem; if no one shares the new strategy, ask, "Did anyone try the method that students in the other class tried?" If no one did, then ask, "How do you think they might have used their strategy to solve this problem?"

---

1. An algorithm is defined as "a precisely specified sequence of steps that will lead to a complete solution" for whichever operation you are working on (Bass 2003, 323). The problem is that the steps of the traditional algorithms have been streamlined so compactly that why they work is hidden from view when students use them. For more on computation and algorithms, see Bass (2003).

- Another strategy we use to nudge students toward reasoning is to say something like "I can see many of you used the traditional algorithm, but when you are trying to figure out something in your head, there are other strategies that are easier to understand and much easier to use. Let's look at this problem. How else could we do this that might be easier? And how else can we think about it? . . . And how else?" Continuing to ask, "How else?" shifts the emphasis from how students have done the problem to other ways they *might* think about it. We have found that this subtle difference can engage the class in thinking differently and creatively together.

Temptations to Resist

Assuming that a student understands why a procedure works or assuming that the traditional algorithm is the best way to do a problem. Expecting students to explain why a standard algorithm works generally isn't productive because most students who learned mathematics as procedures have not been asked to make sense of them in the first place. This is not to say that understanding the logic and mathematical principles underlying these algorithms is not important. Rather, we have found that once children have brought meaning to operations through their own reasoning, the procedures in these traditional algorithms become more readily transparent.

When a student uses the traditional algorithm, it is okay to ask a few "Why?" questions, but, as discussed, you won't want to dwell on the "why" if students revert back to "what." Sometimes we remind students about the goal of Number Talks, saying, for example, "With Number Talks, remember that we are trying to use strategies that we can make sense of and that make it easy to reason with numbers. Can you think of a way to solve this problem that is easier for you?"

Q: Already, in the third week of school, there are a few students who want to share almost every day, while many other students have never shared at all. How can I get more students involved?

A: This happens in every classroom. Some students naturally enjoy sharing their ideas, while others do not. Why? First, talking to the whole class takes experience, which many of our students have not had, and confidence, which many of our students lack. Students may not have an answer or may be afraid their answer is wrong. They may feel a lack of confidence with their English. They may be afraid they won't be able to explain how they got their answer. They may be generally shy. Some students might have had very little experience explaining their ideas at home, while others talk constantly with their parents.

There is much talk about the importance of a safe classroom culture, and we of course agree. Students need to have trust—in the teacher and in the other students in the class—that even their fledgling and incomplete ideas will be respected. But while a safe culture is essential, it is not sufficient to ensure all students' participation.

The dilemma is that explaining and justifying are essential for *all* students. Knowing they can be called on to speak at any moment, though, changes the nature of what people are able to think about. Many students find that the potential to be called on at any moment can easily shift their attention from thinking deeply about the topic under consideration to whether and when they will be chosen to speak, with varying levels of anxiety, depending on how prepared they feel.

We work diligently behind the scenes to encourage reticent students to begin to share their ideas, and even so we are rarely 100 percent successful. But we always work from the premise that all students will have control of whether or not to publicly contribute to the classroom discourse.

Strategies That Have Worked for Us

- We often say, "I would like to hear from someone who hasn't had a chance to share." Then we *wait* . . . and wait some more. You may find that silently counting to ten or twenty helps with what might seem like an interminable amount of time. If no one volunteers after a long wait time, try a different approach, but come back to this strategy in subsequent Number Talks.
- Sometimes bringing a small group of students together in a private Number Talk can be effective in helping them develop confidence in their ability to explain their thinking. Inviting students to share their strategies in a small group can be a safer way for students to learn to share their thinking with others, and they often come to realize that their ideas are valuable. We know this is easier in a self-contained elementary classroom than in a middle school or high school math classroom where students come and go every hour. It is hard to keep track of who is talking and who isn't when you have 150 students. So be patient with yourself, but also be persistent about gradually having a quick individual or small-group Number Talk with students you haven't heard from. Sometimes that's all it takes to get a student to more actively participate in whole-class discussions.
- In classes of painfully reticent older students, some teachers have had success having students share their strategies with a neighbor before the whole class is invited to share. But a caution here is that setting up a situation where all students are expected to share can be frightening for students who are tentative in their thinking, even if they only have to share with one or two other people. Another caution is that if students share their answers before being asked to give answers to the whole class, everyone can

be deprived of the rich possibilities provided by different answers in a Number Talk.

- Sometimes we do a quick formative assessment. First we pose a problem and ask students to mentally solve it two different ways. Then we ask students to record their strategies on both sides of a 3-by-5-inch card. Once everyone is finished, students share within their small groups. Often students who don't speak to the whole class are willing to risk sharing their ideas with a few other students. Smaller groups also offer an easier setting for students to ask questions about another method. When the small-group discussions begin to wind down, we have students put their names on the cards, and we collect them. This short process can also serve as an invaluable formative assessment to help you choose what direction to take in the next Number Talk.

Our bottom line is that we want the learning environment to be safe for all students. Ruth shares,

> I tell my students on the first day of class that I won't put them on the spot but that I will give them lots of opportunities to share their thinking when they choose to. I try hard not to violate this trust. I want the learning environment to be safe for all students. I do talk with kids about how important it is for them to talk about and explain their thinking. With quieter students, I sometimes ask them, one-on-one, to share with me how they thought about a problem. Once they have had a chance to rehearse their thinking with me, I ask them to think about whether they might be willing to share their idea with the class. If they don't choose to, I often ask if they are willing to let me share their idea. Once students have had their own way of thinking recognized and valued, they may become more confident in sharing their ideas.

Some students, despite our best efforts, may never want to share with the whole class, and we have to be okay with that as long as we know that they are learning. That said, Number Talks are one of the safest ways we know to encourage participation.

Temptations to Resist

We've observed some practices over the years that inhibit classroom talk. We have found that avoiding these practices, over time, results in more equitable and thoughtful classroom conversations.

- Allowing children to indicate, or "vote," verbally or nonverbally (for example, with hand signals) when they agree with an answer can be counterproductive. Even though the intention may be to support others, we think this practice places too much emphasis on the answer rather than the problem-solving process, and ultimately can lead to a less safe environment for testing out new ideas.

- While efficiency is foundational for numerical fluency, having students choose the "best" or even "most efficient" strategy can diminish students' willingness to explore and understand new ways of reasoning with numbers. Once students have developed confidence and flexibility with their reasoning, attending to efficiency can be a valuable pursuit.

- Remarks intended to be encouraging, or in any way indicating a preference for one strategy over another, such as "Great!" and "Yes!" put the teacher back in the spotlight. A central goal of Number Talks is to build students' sense of agency and to help us, as teachers, stand aside for students' thinking to take center stage. And of course those students who don't get this kind of response can feel that their contributions are not valued or valuable.

- "Equity sticks" are tempting but counterproductive. See "Guiding Principle 6" in Chapter 3.

- Number Talks that go on too long cause many students to become restless and disengaged. With some exceptions (see Chapter 9), Number Talks should not be longer than about fifteen minutes. This means that sometimes you will need to cut a Number Talk short without hearing from students who want to contribute, but if you are doing Number Talks consistently and frequently, there will always be another chance.

- If Number Talks are sporadic, many students lose the capacity to build on ideas they have had themselves or heard from other students. New ideas are forgotten with gaps in time. Quieter students don't have opportunities to consider new strategies and think about how they work—the kinds of experiences that can build their confidence to try out ideas publicly.

- If Number Talks are to have the intended impact, then purposeful planning must go into selecting problems; otherwise, they can become just another activity. Jumping from one kind of problem to another, and never letting students test out new ideas that they've seen or heard, is unlikely to result in students who can deal flexibly and confidently with numbers. We have written Chapters 4 through 8 to help you with choosing problems that build upon one another.

Q: *What if I get confused or make a mathematical mistake?*

A: This can happen to anyone when mathematical ideas are being explored! For many of us, learning arithmetic was a rote process that rarely offered the opportunity to understand operations and numerical relationships deeply, so it is logical that there will be many soft spots in our own understanding. Number Talks offer us, as well as our students, the opportunity to strengthen our understanding. But, as teachers who have learned that our job is to explain and to be the source of knowledge for students, we may initially panic when we make a mistake or get confused. It isn't comfortable! But cognitive dissonance is necessary for learning—not just for our students. Mistakes—even our own—are truly sites for learning (Hiebert et al. 1997). So we must learn to take a deep breath and embrace the opportunity to model for our students a spirit of wondering, of curiosity, and of being willing to embrace and examine our mistakes in a search for meaning. We have found that it is beneficial for our students to see their teacher's comfort with being confused or wrong. We have often invited our students to help us figure out what was wrong with our thinking or our recording of an idea and have found that students of all ages willingly rise to the occasion.

Strategies That Have Worked for Us
- "Yikes. I think there is something wrong here. Can anyone help me figure this out?"
- "Uh-oh. I just confused myself. Hmm—where am I? Can anyone help me think about this?"
- "I think I have just made a mistake—my synapses are firing!"
- "I'm going to think about this overnight, and I hope you will help me think about it. We'll talk about it tomorrow and try to figure it out."

Temptations to Resist
Being embarrassed about our mistakes or trying to cover them up or make excuses for them—or saying we made a mistake "on purpose"—sends the wrong message. We are models for our students, and if we want our students to learn from their mistakes, we have to be willing to do the same. The key is being open and honest with students.

Q: I know we are supposed to use mistakes as sites for learning, but what should we do when a student's answer—or method—is wrong?

A: Sometimes as many as four—or more—different answers emerge from a Number Talk. Some arise from small computation errors, while others indicate misconceptions about how a property or operation works. These latter errors are the ones that offer the greatest opportunity for moving students' understanding of mathematics forward. Our goal here is to get our students to the point where they are genuinely curious, rather than embarrassed, about their mistakes.

Strategies That Have Worked for Us

- We establish a class norm that any answer, right or wrong, must be justified. A student explaining a strategy should begin with identifying the answer he or she is defending. "Which answer are you defending?" is a good prompt for this and communicates that the logic of the mathematics will determine whether a strategy is sound.
- Usually it becomes apparent early on which answer is "right." There are several possible ways to approach the other answers if you decide it would be valuable to discuss them. You can ask, "Is the person who answered _____ willing to tell us how you thought about this?" If no one volunteers, you can just let it go, or you might want to ask, "How might someone arrive at this answer?" If there is a lingering question about which answer is right, you might want to say about the strategy or strategies, "Let's try this with smaller numbers that we know the answer to and see if it works."
- Another approach is to turn the mistake into a class investigation (see Chapter 9).

Temptations to Resist

- Resist acknowledging, verbally or nonverbally, that an answer is right or wrong, especially before your students have had a chance to examine and defend the various answers. This may seem, for some of you, like educational malpractice. Isn't it a teacher's job to help students know where they have gone wrong? The reality, though, is that as students listen to different ways of solving the problems, they will notice their errors on their own, and they will work to correct their thinking. It is important to give them a chance to do this. Again, once a safe environment has been established, it is okay to ask, "Does anyone who now knows their answer is wrong want to share what you did?" If you don't get volunteers, though, it is important not to put individual students on the spot.

Q: *What do I do if I don't know how to record a student's thinking?*

A: Recording is trickier than it looks, and it isn't an exact science. The main thing is to write just enough so that the class can clearly "see" how a student's strategy works. Write too little and we probably haven't pressed the student enough for why their method makes sense; write too much, and the student's thinking gets muddled and/or hard for others to follow.

There are many effective ways to record, but because the recording issues are a little different for each operation, we have included examples of ways to record students' thinking in each operations chapter (see Chapters 4 through 8). We hope you will find these useful as you experiment with what works for you.

Strategies That Have Worked for Us

We have found that it helps to listen to a student for a while before we start writing, in order to get the gist of the strategy or where the mathematics is going. Sometimes we erase what we have written as a student talks and start all over again. If we get really stuck on how to record the strategy, we say so, and occasionally even invite the student to come to the document camera or board to show the strategy.

Q: *How do I get buy-in from my high school students?*

A: Number Talks help students of all ages become responsible for their own reasoning. But high school students have had a long time to practice what they believe to be their responsibilities in math class; typically, these include listening closely to the teacher so they will know how to follow steps for "the" way to solve a problem. But Number Talks change the rules for what is expected of them. When a teacher asks, "Why does that make sense?" students can become bewildered, mixing up what *makes sense* with what they are supposed to *do*. Sometimes they become frustrated that, all of a sudden, knowing what to do isn't enough.

Unfortunately, there is no magic wand to help students realize that making sense of what they do empowers them to be able to use mathematics in many situations. So, as you help students along this path, one important thing to remember is that success is a great motivator, and nothing feels quite as good as really understanding something. That said, we have found a couple of things that can help hook students' interest and shift their thinking.

Strategies That Have Worked for Us

- First, we have found that starting with "dot talks" (see the classroom lesson in Chapter 2) is very valuable for all students, from elementary through high school. Dot talks do not carry the baggage of an arithmetic operation. It is fun to visualize the dots, and the students get experience with the important mathematical practice of clearly explaining their thinking in a low-risk setting. This is also an important initial step in helping students understand that people see—and think—in different ways. More importantly, dot talks level the playing field, so to speak. People see differently, and everyone can talk about what they see. Several dot talks, not just one, lay a firmer foundation for using mathematical practices in a no-risk environment.

- Second, we have seen teachers catch older students' attention with contexts they relate to, as with the milkshake math problem mentioned earlier. We also have seen teachers occasionally embed Number Talks in other contexts; one teacher, for example, did a Number Talk involving subtracting from 90 degrees or 180 degrees when her class was studying complementary and supplementary angles. On the other hand, if you want to spend just fifteen minutes in Number Talks, you will often want to present computation problems without a context (so-called naked-number problems) so that the entire focus is on how numbers and operations work and why. When you do use a context for Number Talks, it should not be so complex as to draw students' attention away from working with numbers.
- A final word about buy-in: patience. Don't give up. Keep the talks short, less than fifteen minutes, so that they hold students' attention. And be encouraging; success is a great motivator.

Temptations to Resist

Giving in and giving up. Number Talks provide a foundation with numerical and algebraic reasoning, and there is too much to be gained to give up on them, on your kids, or on yourself.

Number Talks help to establish a culture where students are expected to make sense of mathematics in their own ways, learn to defend their ideas mathematically, and learn to listen to and build on the thinking of their peers. These characteristics are the essence of the *mathematical practices*, the characteristics and dispositions that will prepare students for future success with mathematics, for college, and for their careers.

> **Q: *My Number Talks are going pretty well, but they still seem to be two-way communications between me and a student (T-S-T-S-T-S). How can I get students to listen and talk to one another?***

A: This question gets to the heart of Number Talks. Our goal is to help students learn to make mathematically convincing arguments in support of their ideas and listen to and build on one another's ideas. This often means that we need to work purposefully to change the pattern of our interactions with students and theirs with one another.

Strategies That Have Worked for Us

- Orient students to others' thinking by asking questions like "What questions do you have for Miki?" or "Do you think Ellie's method will work every time? Talk to her about what you think." When hands are raised, don't call on a student yourself, but rather, say, "_____, there are some kids who want to talk to you." Then let the one sharing the strategy call on someone.

- You can help your students learn to ask, "Does anybody have a question?" or "Does that make sense to you?" after they have shared a way of thinking. If a student is willing to share something he or she is not sure about, this is something to be celebrated.
- You can respond by saying, "_____ is not sure her idea makes sense, so she's asking for our help, so pay careful attention here." We want to build a community of learners where students know that we are all in this together, trying to learn new ways of working efficiently with numbers.

Temptations to Resist

Being too quick to respond. Students are used to waiting for us to respond to ideas, and we're used to responding. It's important to wait after a student shares to give other students a chance to think about questions they might have. This wait time also allows the student sharing to think about his or her response and perhaps refine it.

Q: *One of the hardest things for me is knowing what questions to ask! How can I get past, "Who thought about it a different way?"*

A: This is another important question. Number Talks are not really about how many ways problems are solved; they are about understanding how students make sense of the problems we pose. The questions we ask can help students come to value this as they learn to ask questions of one another.

Strategies That Have Worked for Us

- After a student has shared a strategy, we often ask if anyone solved it the same way, noting students' responses. As mentioned, we also ask the students, "What questions do you have for _____?" We first listen to students' questions before asking our own. When students don't ask any questions of one another, we often say, "Well, I have a question," then we ask questions like "Why did you do _____?" or "Can you explain what you were thinking here?" Even though we might fully understand a strategy that has been shared, we often think about important ideas in the strategy that might be confusing to some students; for example, we would ask a purposeful question such as "Why did you add four here?" when a student has subtracted a multiple of ten and then added some back.
- We also sometimes ask students to consider what is similar and/or different about two strategies that have been shared by their classmates.

Kathy Richardson, who developed the practice of Number Talks with Ruth and first named them "Number Talks," says,

> The power in the Number Talks comes from inspiring each child to think and make sense of the mathematics they are presented. They are never trying to figure out what the teacher wants. Rather, they are totally engaged in their own sense-making process. . . . A Number Talk is an opportunity for children to learn that they can figure things out for themselves in the way that makes sense to them. This is the true meaning of "lifelong learner." (www.mathperspectives.com)

We know that once you are on your way, you are likely to find that often during Number Talks your students are teaching you and their classmates more than you are teaching them, which does wonders for their sense of themselves as mathematical thinkers.

Probably the most important thing you can do for yourself is to find a colleague to collaborate and talk with as you embark on this journey. While there will likely be bumps in the road, over time, the benefits to you, your students, and your classroom as a community will far outweigh the challenges.

11 Moving Forward

In this book, we have shared with you our deepest beliefs about teaching and learning along with what we hope is enough practical guidance to help you get started with and sustain this transformative practice. We hope you are excited to begin Number Talks or take them to the next level in your classroom, and confident enough to keep them going. Remember that this is not about changing your whole math program—just fifteen minutes of each day. And the more frequently you incorporate those fifteen minutes into your regular instruction, the more your students' mathematical ideas will propel everyone's learning forward.

We think of Number Talks as offering a dedicated space for students' ideas, and you will delight in ongoing surprises as students come to share their ideas freely. When you shift away from teaching "what to do" to encouraging students to think in their own ways; away from teaching procedures for students to practice to posing problems and letting kids grapple with them; and away from knowing what you want students to say to listening with honest curiosity to the things they have to say, then your teaching and life in your classroom will be forever changed.

You've heard a lot from us, so now we'd like you to hear from among the many students and teachers who have shared with us their experiences with Number Talks.

It takes a lot more productive mathematical strength to invent a strategy and test it than it does to memorize a procedure. I believe Number Talks are a powerful, painless, threat-free way to explore mathematics where students talk mathematics, reason mathematically, and develop a strong sense of number. I will always use them in my classes.—*Donna, mathematics instructor, University of Alabama at Birmingham*

Many students are at first anxious and nervous to complete the Number Talks, but their skills slowly grow, and they begin to pick up on their peers' strategies, eventually adopting the most efficient methods. For my classroom and students, Number Talks serve as an avenue for discussing what mathematics is, how we can communicate in math, and how we can learn from each other to build our understanding about mathematical concepts.—*Tara, high school teacher, New Mexico*

During my seventeen years of working with high school students and adult learners, I have observed a nearly unanimous lack of comfort with and/or understanding of basic arithmetic. Even students who are fluent with standard algorithms very rarely understand how they work or why they are valid. Worse yet, they fail to see why caring about such a thing would even be important. This failure to expect of themselves a deeper level of understanding pervades every aspect of their work in even the highest levels of mathematics courses. Number Talks address this issue in a more direct and efficient way than I'd have thought possible.

I have found that students of widely varying backgrounds and levels of comfort with mathematics are equally engaged and challenged during Number Talks, no matter the apparent difficulty of the problem at hand. It is extremely rare to find a mathematical activity that so efficiently evens the playing field for students and cuts right to what may very well be at the core of our challenges as mathematics educators: the widely accepted belief of students (and I would argue many educators as well) that the ability to accurately and efficiently repeat an impressive list of algorithms constitutes a high-quality learning of mathematics. Students and educators both grow immensely when this belief is so authentically challenged.—*Debbie, mathematics instructor, Spokane Falls Community College, Washington*

At first I was just doing [mathematics] the traditional way, but now that I have seen how others think of the problems, it can be easier. I think I am smarter for making it simpler and understanding it. Plus, I can get it even faster.—*Javier, high school junior, Santa Clara Valley, California*

I started Number Talks with my intervention class, and it has quickly become my students' very favorite part of class. They come in and the first thing they ask is if we are going to do a Number Talk that day. It's pretty awesome hearing students' different ways of thinking about a problem, and it astounds them as to how many ways there are to solve a problem.—*Nisha, seventh- and eighth-grade teacher, Washington*

This showed me new ways of thinking about problems and helped me realize what I was doing *while* I was doing problems. And I am amazed by what is in my brain and what I can do in my head. At first I only did the traditional algorithm. Once I was looking at it with different views, I was amazed that I could think, "Well, 5 percent of $100 is $5, so 5 percent of $200 is $10."—*Andie, high school sophomore, San Francisco Bay Area*

Just a week into school I have a couple of ELL students that have even been willing to share already, which is pretty great.—*Mark, sixth-grade teacher, Washington*

At the beginning of the school year, students struggle with being able to explain their thinking by only using their words. A lot of students want to write their thought process on the board, but by requiring them to explain using only verbal communication, they are able to form their thoughts better. Over time, the students' explanations improve along with their confidence. The students also became better listeners. They seem to feel motivated to listen to one another not only because they are required to but also because they are interested in other students' methods. I always encouraged them to try a method from a previous Number Talk, and the students had no problem doing so.

Finally, the students' number sense improved. I could see the improvement during non–Number Talk class time. Specifically, while doing a warm-up, students began solving the problems in the Number Talk fashion, rather than doing traditional algorithms. They became quite efficient at mental arithmetic, and I completely attribute this to Number Talks. Geometry classwork was impacted, as well, because multiple methods became a norm. Students were zealous when it came to sharing their methods. Overall, Number Talks have created a classroom culture of sharing ideas, listening to one another, and becoming more flexible math thinkers.—*Melissa, high school teacher, Los Angeles, California*

I have been seeing many more students interested in sharing their ideas than I did on the first day, and I have only been doing them [Number Talks] for four days!—*Suzy, fifth-grader teacher, Washington*

I think the primary value is that Number Talks foster a safe classroom environment. First, by not tying the activity to "today's content," and thus the insecurities of feeling underwater in the class, there are a wider number of people who feel confident enough to share.—*David, high school teacher, San Francisco Bay Area*

In my first two years of teaching, I used Number Talks inconsistently and fit them in when I had time. However, this year I built time into my daily schedule for Number Talks, and I have seen amazing results! Many students (including those already strong in math) who came to me with very little number sense and place value understanding are now easily manipulating numbers and using them to solve problems in different ways. I have seen a significant impact in the mathematical dispositions of my students. They enjoy math more (even asking for more Number Talks) and are more willing to spend time thinking about problems rather than immediately asking for help. In regard to other subject areas, I have noticed my students looking for patterns in everything we do. They are using the critical thinking skills required in Number Talks to analyze the books they are reading, science experiments, and their writing.—*Amanda, third-grade teacher, Alabama*

We included this last comment from a third-grade teacher to help you realize that, over time, more and more students who are experienced with Number Talks will come to you from classrooms like Amanda's. When they do, getting Number Talks started will be much easier because you will not have to work so hard to convince students that there are different ways to think about problems or that it really is safe to share their ideas.

It will be quite a journey as you work with your students to really make Number Talks matter. Yes, there will be struggles—but don't give up! Find several colleagues to collaborate with and support you along the way. Remember, these are big changes for you and your students. Real and lasting change takes time and practice. Once you're on your way, we're quite certain you'll never turn back, and you will find the work to be profoundly rewarding. So be sure to enjoy the journey!

Appendix A

Planning a Number Talk

Anticipate different strategies students might use for solving the problem (or how they might "see" a dot card).	How will you record each of these strategies?
What questions might you ask to fully understand and represent a student's thinking and/or method?	In reflecting on this Number Talk, what do you want to remember, what problem might you do next, and why?

Appendix B

Properties of Operations on Rational Numbers

Properties of Addition

Commutative Property of Addition: $a + b = b + a$

$$2 + 3 = 3 + 2$$

Associative Property of Addition: $(a + b) + c = a + (b + c)$

$$(2 + 3) + 4 = 2 + (3 + 4)$$

Existence of Identity: The number 0 satisfies $a + 0 = a = 0 + a$

$$3 + 0 = 3 = 0 + 3$$

Existence of Additive Inverse: For any rational number a, there exists $-a$ such that $a + (-a) = 0$

$$2 + (-2) = 0$$

Properties of Multiplication

Commutative Property of Multiplication: $a \times b = b \times a$

$$2 \times 3 = 3 \times 2$$

Associative Property of Multiplication: $(a \times b) \times c = a \times (b \times c)$

$$(2 \times 3) \times 4 = 2 \times (3 \times 4)$$

Existence of Identity: $a \times 1 = 1 \times a = a$

$$3 \times 1 = 1 \times 3 = 3$$

Existence of Multiplicative Inverse: For every nonzero rational number a, there exists $\frac{1}{a}$ such that $a \times \frac{1}{a} = 1$

$$2 \times \frac{1}{2} = \frac{1}{2} \times 2 = 1$$

Linking Multiplication and Addition: The Ninth Property

Distributive Property of Multiplication over Addition: $a \times (b + c) = (a \times b) + (a \times c)$

$$a(b+c) = ab + ac$$

$$3(2+5) = 3(2) + 3(5)$$

Appendix C

Dot Cards

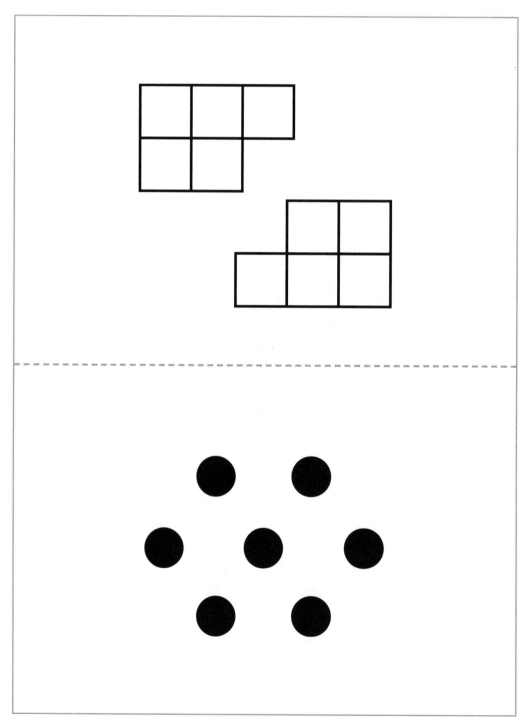

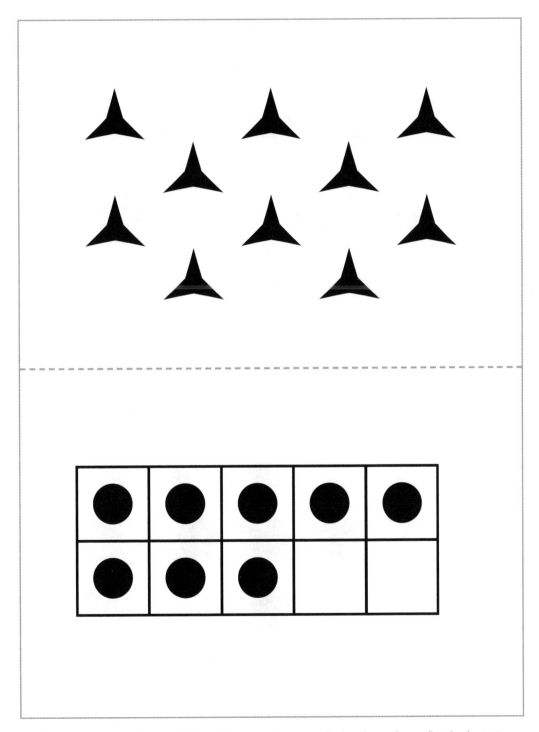

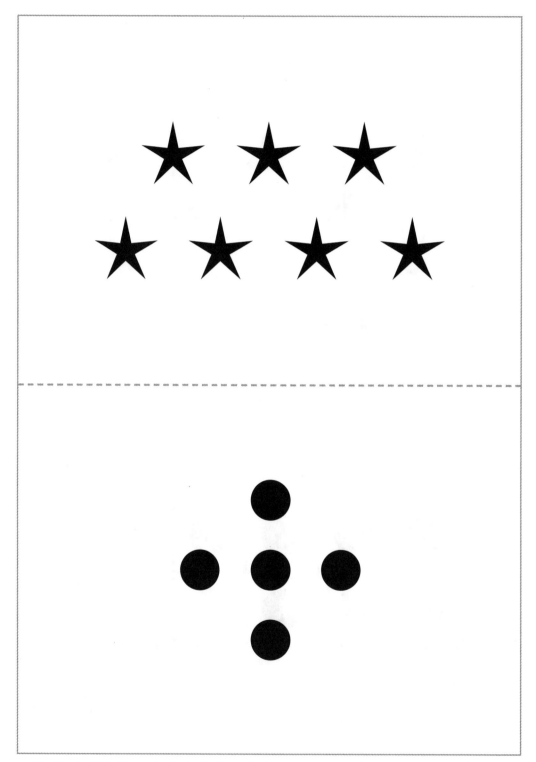

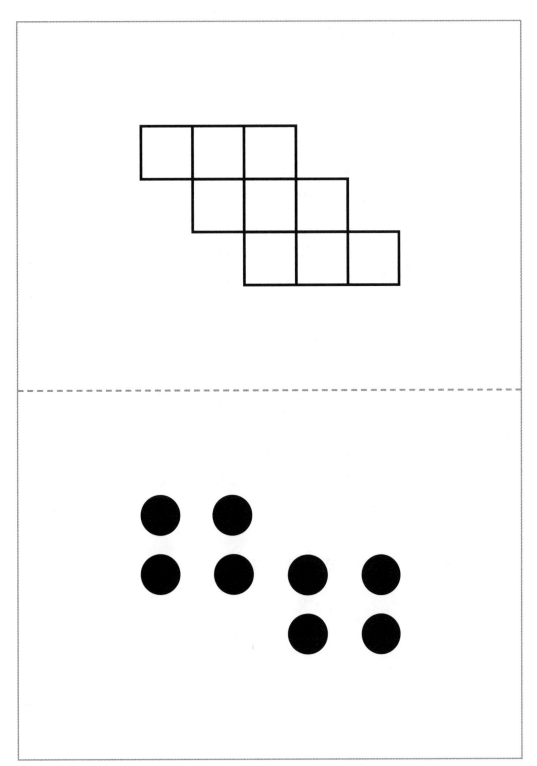

Strategies for Subtraction

61 − 27

- Adding up (represent with and without the open number line)

- Breaking apart the subtrahend (represent with and without the open number line)

- Adding the same quantity to the subtrahend and the minuend (represent with and without the open number line)

- Rounding the subtrahend to the nearest multiple of 10 (or 100, 1000, etc.) and compensating

- Using negative numbers

Play Around with These

Play around with these problems **using the main strategies** for subtraction. Which strategies work efficiently? Try not to use any "rules" you know.

$$7.46 - 6.85 \qquad 60.12 - 0.2$$

$$8.2 - .97 \qquad 3\tfrac{1}{4} - 1\tfrac{5}{8}$$

$$3\tfrac{1}{5} - 2\tfrac{4}{5} \qquad -5 - (-9)$$

$$-3 - 2$$

References

Bass, Hyman. 2003. "Computational Fluency, Algorithms, and Mathematical Proficiency: One Mathematician's Perspective." *Teaching Children Mathematics* 9 (6): 322–327.

Beilock, Sian. 2011. *Choke: What the Secrets of the Brain Reveal About Getting It Right When You Have To.* New York: Simon and Schuster, Free Press.

Boaler, Jo. 2008. *What's Math Got to Do with It?* New York: Viking Penguin.

———. 2014. "Research Suggests That Timed Tests Cause Math Anxiety." *Teaching Children Mathematics* 20 (8): 469–474.

Boaler, Jo, and Cathy Humphreys. 2005. *Connecting Mathematical Ideas: Middle School Video Cases to Support Teaching and Learning.* Portsmouth, NH: Heinemann.

Burns, Marilyn. 1984. *The Math Solution: Teaching Mathematics Through Problem Solving.* Sausalito, CA: Marilyn Burns Education Associates.

———. 2007. *About Teaching Mathematics: A K–8 Resource.* 3rd ed. Sausalito, CA: Math Solutions.

California State Department of Education. 1988. *Mathematics Model Curriculum Guide: Kindergarten Through Grade Eight.* Sacramento, CA: California State Department of Education.

Carpenter, Thomas, Megan Franke, and Linda Levi. 2003. *Thinking Mathematically: Integrating Arithmetic and Algebra in Elementary School.* Portsmouth, NH: Heinemann.

Daro, Phil. 2010. "The Common Core State Standards: Make the Difference." National Council of Supervisors of Mathematics Annual Conference, San Diego, California, April 19–21.

———. 2014. "Teaching and Learning in the Era of the Common Core State Standards and Assessments." National Council of Supervisors of Mathematics Annual Conference, New Orleans, Louisiana, April 7–9.

Duckworth, Eleanor. 1987. "The Having of Wonderful Ideas." In *"The Having of Wonderful Ideas" and Other Essays on Teaching and Learning.* New York: Teachers College Press.

Dweck, Carol. 2006. *Mindset: The New Psychology of Success.* New York: Random House.

Fosnot, Catherine Twomey, and Martin Dolk. 2001. *Young Mathematicians at Work: Constructing Multiplication and Division.* Portsmouth, NH: Heinemann.

———. 2002. *Young Mathematicians at Work: Constructing Fractions, Decimals, and Percents.* Portsmouth, NH: Heinemann.

Harris, Pamela. 2011. *Building (Powerful) Numeracy for Middle and High School Students.* Portsmouth, NH: Heinemann.

Hiebert, James. 1999. "Relationships Between Research and the NCTM Standards." *Journal for Research in Mathematics Education* 30 (1): 3–19.

Hiebert, James, Thomas Carpenter, Elizabeth Fennema, Karen Fuson, Diana Wearne, Hanlie Murray, Alwyn Olivier, and Piet Human. 1997. *Making Sense: Teaching and Learning Mathematics with Understanding*. Portsmouth, NH: Heinemann.

Kamii, Constance. 2000. *Young Children Reinvent Arithmetic: Implications of Piaget's Theory*. New York: Teachers College Press.

Kazemi, Elham. 1998. "Discourse That Promotes Conceptual Understanding." *Teaching Children Mathematics* 4 (7): 410–414.

Kazemi, Elham, and Allison Hintz. 2014. *Intentional Talk: How to Structure and Lead Productive Mathematical Discussions*. Portland, ME: Stenhouse.

Kliman, Marlene, Susan Jo Russell, Cornelia Tierney, and Megan Murray. 1996. *Building on Numbers You Know: Computation and Estimation Strategies, Grade 5*. Palo Alto, CA: Dale Seymour Publications.

Labinowicz, Ed. 1980. *The Piaget Primer: Thinking, Learning, Teaching*. Palo Alto, CA: Dale Seymour Publications.

Lane County Mathematics Project. 1983a. *Problem Solving in Mathematics, Grade 7*. Palo Alto, CA: Dale Seymour Publications.

———. 1983b. *Problem Solving in Mathematics, Grade 8*. Palo Alto, CA: Dale Seymour Publications.

Ma, Liping. 1999. *Knowing and Teaching Elementary Mathematics*. Mahwah, NJ: Erlbaum.

Maier, Eugene. 1982. "Long Division Dead as a Dodo Bird." The Math Learning Center. http://www.mathlearningcenter.org/resources/gene/archive/long_division_dead.

Mathematics Education Collaborative. 2006. *Multiplication: Helping Your Children Know Their Basic Facts*. From the Supporting School Mathematics: How to Work with Parents and the Public series. Portsmouth, NH: Heinemann.

Moschkovich, Judit. 1999. "Supporting the Participation of English Language Leaners in Mathematical Discussions." *For the Learning of Mathematics* 19 (1): 11–19.

National Council of Teachers of Mathematics. 1989. *Curriculum and Evaluation Standards for School Mathematics*. Reston, VA: National Council of Teachers of Mathematics.

National Governors Association Center for Best Practices and Council of Chief State School Officers. 2010. *Common Core State Standards for Mathematics*. Washington, DC: National Governors Association Center for Best Practices and Council of Chief State School Officers.

Reys, Robert, Paul Trafton, Barbara Reys, and Judy Zawojewski. 1987. *Computational Estimation, Grade 7*. Palo Alto, CA: Dale Seymour Publications.

Richardson, Kathy. 2011. "What Is the Distinction Between a Lesson and a Number Talk?" Math Perspectives Teacher Development Center. http://www.mathperspectives.com/pdf_docs/mp_lesson_ntalks_distinction.pdf.

Rowe, Mary Budd. 1986. "Wait Time: Slowing Down May Be a Way of Speeding Up." *Journal of Teacher Education* 37: 43–50.

Sawyer, Walter Warwick. 1961. *A Mathematician's Delight*. London: Penguin.

Tobias, Sheila. 1978. *Overcoming Math Anxiety*. New York: W.W. Newton and Company.

Van de Walle, John, and Lou Ann H. Lovin. 2006. *Teaching Student-Centered Mathematics, Grades 5–8*. Boston, MA: Allyn and Bacon.

Index